While You Were Micro-Sleeping

Fresh Insights on the Changing Face of North American Missions

by Steve Moore

THE MISSION EXCHANGE

© 2009 Steve Moore

Published by The Mission Exchange in association with Snowfall Press.

ISBN: 978-0-615-33222-2

Library of Congress Control Number: 2009940951

Cover design and layout by Marcel Venter | FreshBrand.com

Dedicated to: Don Bray, without your mentor sponsorship I would never have engaged this amazing adventure, and the risk taking radicals of The Mission Exchange (then EFMA) Presidential Search Committee and Board of Directors, who in the face of all conventional wisdom gave me the privilege and opportunity to serve the Great Commission community in this role.

ACKNOWLEDGEMENTS

Special thanks to Joe Trimmer for volunteering the time and expertise needed to record our monthly vlog segments. Your passion for film and desire to leverage your giftedness for the kingdom is refreshing.

Thanks to Brian Tetamore at TheVisualChurch.com for adding your masterful post-production touch to our vlog each month. Your heart for the kingdom and spirit of generosity is a great blessing.

Thanks to 12Stone Church for making space in the café and allowing Joe to use such quality equipment.

Thanks to our amazing team at The Mission Exchange for all you do to support the crazy ideas, including a video blog, that arrive in a flash but take hours of work to carry out.

CONTENTS

CHAPTER ONE
A METAPHOR OF
MISSIONS TODAY

If you ordered this book from the online store in our web site the physical product you hold in your hands did not exist in this form when you clicked on the button authorizing us to charge your credit card and confirm your purchase. Immediately after your transaction was complete you received an email confirmation of your order from our web site, and simultaneously we were notified of your purchase.

Your order was forwarded to Snowfall Press, which activated their internal processes and in a matter of seconds[1] a single copy of *While You Were Micro-Sleeping,* the one you are now reading, began printing. In less than twenty minutes it was bound and dropped into a mailing envelope just for you.

No inventory. No warehouse. No problem.

This is Gutenberg on steroids. Or perhaps it is where Gutenberg meets Google, the confluence of physical, digital and virtual.

I recognize the quality associated with on-demand printing is not yet on par with traditional methods. But that will change in time, perhaps faster than you think. (Maybe while you are micro-sleeping.) One could easily imagine a world where digital books dominate with print editions only surfacing on-demand.

Some books will exist in multiple forms simultaneously as a series of blog or vlog posts on a web site, individual PDF files by chapter and the on-demand print version. Mass customization is no longer a competitive advantage but a customer expectation. In compilation books like this one, individuals will insist they be allowed to order only the chapters they want, organized (in terms of the order of chapters) in the way that makes sense to the reader. (In fact, we could have taken that approach with this book but opted for the old school, one-size fits all, on-demand print edition.)

---

[1] This is assuming the printer is not already engaged with another job and there is nothing in the print queue ahead of your order.

Interesting, but what does all this have to do with missions? A lot.

What Mission Agencies can Learn from the World of Publishing

There was a day when the only pathway to publishing a book ran through a publishing company. If you wanted to author a book you did whatever you could to get the attention of a publisher who served as an iron clad gatekeeper for your ideas. If the publisher liked your material and believed you were a "marketable personality," you might get a book deal. As the importance of being a marketable personality has increased, a number of publishers simply stopped accepting unsolicited manuscripts. The iron clad gate is now locked.

To be fair, publishers need to make money or they can't keep publishing books. And recognizing books that people will want to read is not an exact science. Almost every successful author who did not start out as a marketable personality has a story to tell about the dozens of rejection notices he or she received from publishers who walked away from a wildly successful manuscript after having deemed it unworthy of taking up space on the bookstore shelf.

But the world is changing and so are the rules. With the proliferation of desktop computers, desktop publishing and lower cost printing, there are ways to self-publish a book that completely circumvent the world of traditional publishing. If you have a good idea, the ability to write, access to a decent editor, a creative graphic designer and a few thousand dollars to spend for printing, you can produce your own book whether the publishing world wants you to or not. If you are willing to go print on demand, you don't even need the few thousand dollars. The iron clad gate might be locked but it doesn't matter; it is no longer necessary to go through that door.

I have seen a number of self-published books (including hardcover) in the past few years that are of such good quality they could be smuggled on to a shelve at Barnes and Noble and no one would think the book was out of place until the person at the sales register called for a price check. One of the self-published books I came across last year is in the top ten leadership books I've read in recent memory. I've purchased it by the case and given it out everywhere. But only after the book was already in print by way of a self-published edition did traditional publishers take notice. Now all of the sudden[2] this author is worthy of a multiple book deal.

Of course not all authors are able to leverage their self-published books into a relationship with a traditional publisher. For many, the exhilaration that

---

[2] I know the "proper" form of this idiom is "all of a sudden" but it is very possible common usage of "all of the sudden" will become the acceptable form soon. We are using "all of the sudden" throughout this book as a reminder the world is constantly changing and people working outside the "system" don't always have to follow "the rules."

comes when they pull that first book out of the case and see their name on the cover wanes quickly as they struggle to figure out how to move the five thousand copies now sitting in the corner of their garage.

Motivated authors who are also speakers try to book events and promote back of the room sales. The other option is to sell the book over the Internet via a homegrown web site and make it available through online vendors like Amazon.com. But eventually most self-published authors realize traditional publishers have distribution channels and marketing mechanisms they don't have and are not likely to develop on their own.

A Metaphor for Missions

These changes in the world of publishing serve as a metaphor for what is happening in the world of North American missions. There was a day when individuals or churches who wanted to make a difference around the world had little choice but to work with and through traditional mission structures. If you wanted to find out what was happening in the world you were to a large extent dependent on what agencies told you with very few options for exploring another point of view.

In the same way that desktop computers and desktop publishing changed the rules for publishing companies, more efficient and cost effective travel, 24/7 cable news services and broadband Internet has changed the rules for mission agencies. Your constituents are no longer dependent on you for information. Like self-published authors, Christ-followers and churches can carry out their grassroots Great Commission agenda in ways that completely circumvent traditional systems and structures. Like it or not, the rules are changing. Forever. (More on this in chapter 6.)

Traditional publishers tend to look down on self-published authors. There is an elitism that goes beyond protecting market share and profitability. Sometimes this "look-down-your-nose" attitude is subliminal, sometimes it is blatant. (More on this in chapter 8.) There is a tendency to scoff at the leading edge of technology as being inferior, which is how many in the publishing and printing world will react when they see this book in the on demand format. The unspoken (or not) reaction is, "If so and so had something to say and could string two sentences together he would have worked with a real publisher and produced a real book." Unless of course the book goes viral in the self-published form and then all of the sudden a loser becomes a genius overnight. (More on this in chapter 7.)

Mission agencies are a lot like traditional publishers. The assumption is that our field is highly sophisticated, extremely technical and it's just not possible for someone working outside the structures and systems to contribute much value to the cause. Publishers have managing editors; we have missiologists. Both are highly trained experts who know a bad idea when they see one. (Please don't write me about this, I love missiology.)

This line of thinking is not completely off base. The easier it gets to self publish, the more the marketplace of ideas is diluted and the harder it is for consumers to determine trusted sources of quality. Some of these wannabe authors are engaging in narcissistic self-aggrandizement that is not worth the proverbial paper it was printed on, in bulk or one book at a time. Similarly, some maverick missionary adventures are ill advised expressions of the Amazing Race with a Bible. It would be bad enough if we only had to lament the misuse of kingdom funds when poorly trained and culturally insensitive short-termers head for the field. The larger and longer term problem is the potential setback for incarnational workers whose ministry is negatively affected by well intentioned but unprepared teams. (Don't write me about this either; I love short-term missions.)

Problems of this nature are almost inevitable when opportunity is democratized. It is just as foolish for mission agency leaders as it is for publishers to hunker down in an elitist bunker looking for ways to put the cat back in the box. It is not going to happen. (More on this in chapter 2.) On the contrary we need to devise better ways to identify the grassroots initiatives that have game-changing potential for the Great Commission. We need to embrace paradigm busting ideas that redefine how traditional structures work together with viable grass roots initiatives. (More on this in chapter 4.)

This will require courage and risk. It will call forth a new kind of leader who refuses to hide behind concerns about brand identity (who will get the credit if it works?) and quality control (who will take the blame if it fails?), and focuses instead on opportunities that have never existed before. (More on this in chapter 2 and chapter 7.)

Inasmuch as agencies can be a lot like publishers, grassroots mission activists can be a lot like self-published authors. It is one thing to publish your own book, it is something else to market it effectively or produce it in different formats or work through the process of licensing it internationally. Like authors with a few thousand books in the corner of the garage, some grassroots activists are recognizing mission agencies do have expertise that could be helpful and it would be foolish to spend years making mistakes from which others have already learned.

We circumvented the traditional publishing world to produce this book not only because it was faster, gave us more control and could be stored digitally until you pressed "purchase" on our web site. *We pursued this on demand approach because it is in itself a powerful metaphor for the changing face of North American missions.*

Like traditional publishers working with self-published authors, the challenge for mission agencies comes in finding the people who are working outside the system but have something important to contribute and figuring out how to help them go to the next level. I believe this is a metaphor for missions and a lesson both agencies and churches can learn from the world of publishing.

Learning @ the Speed of Life

The world is changing so rapidly, leaders who stop learning for even the shortest period of time dance with underachievement and irrelevance. In an attempt to call attention to this issue I launched a monthly video blog in September 2008 called Learning @ the Speed of Life. We designed this free monthly resource to communicate what is happening at The Mission Exchange, including our webinars, books we are profiling in Leader's Edge Book Summary, the author we interviewed for that month in Leader's Edge Audio Extra and to share a few ideas I hope will give you something to think about, maybe even talk over with your team. (More on all this on pages 35-38.)

We post a new vlog (that's short for video blog) on the 5th of every month. I really had no idea how well our vlog would be received when we launched it. We've been amazed and encouraged by the response of individuals who watch as well as reports of teams viewing together. In one case, denominational leaders included a vlog post as part of their planning retreat; we've even heard from a mission trainer who used vlogs to augment workshops he was presenting in Asia.

Amidst all this positive feedback we heard comments like, "I enjoy the vlog but I could more readily harvest these ideas for future reference if it was available in printed form." Others have suggested it would be easier to get peers and colleagues to wrestle with these important topics of they could hand them a book and say, "It's all thought provoking but we *definitely* need to engage with the content in chapter X."

Since customer feedback is very important at The Mission Exchange, we've responded by putting the transcripts from our monthly vlog in book form.

The title of my very first vlog was *While You Were Micro-Sleeping* and after looking at the general tone and theme of the monthly posts, we decided to make it the title of the book. In most vlog posts there is a focus on how the world of missions is changing for North Americans, hence the subtitle: *The*

Changing Face of North American Missions. Over the course of the year the length of my vlog posts varied from about six minutes to more like ten (OK twelve in a few cases).

That obviously suggests some scripts are slightly longer than others. To compensate where needed I have added some content that was not originally in the vlog to keep the length of chapters consistent. This extra content is in the form of a sidebar so you can see at a glance how the actual video in our vlog archive would differ from content in the chapter if you chose to show it to a group as part of a training or planning session.

Just like our monthly edition of Learning @ the Speed of Life, as you read these chapters I hope we give you something to think about, maybe even talk over with your team.

CHAPTER TWO
WHILE YOU WERE MICRO-SLEEPING

Have you ever had a conversation with someone who was giving you directions that took you through a small town and they tried to help you understand how really small the community was by warning you, "Don't blink or you'll miss it?" That is an interesting metaphor for the challenges church and mission leaders face given the accelerated pace of change in our world.

I realize most small towns have reduced speed limits when you enter them, but think about this: if you were traveling at seventy miles an hour and closed your eyes for three seconds, you would go just over one-hundred yards before you re-engaged with your surroundings. If you are more interested in sports than math, that's an entire football field.

This three second episode is technically called a micro-sleep. But here's what I find really interesting: experts say micro-sleeps often occur without us even knowing what happened! In fact, micro-sleeps can happen while our eyes are still wide open but we fail to respond to outside information. That's begging for a leadership application.

Jack Welch once said if the pace of change inside your organization is not greater than the pace of change outside your organization then the end is near. You may not agree with him, but the point is loud and clear. Someone in your organization needs to be paying attention to what's happening around you so you can respond to outside information.

The disciples were micro-sleeping their way thru Samaria in John 4, which explains why Jesus said, "Open your eyes and look at the fields! They are ripe for harvest." (John 4:35) Jesus had proven the fields were ripe by his conversation with the woman at the well. But the disciples were not responsive to what God was doing around them.

To remain relevant and effective, leaders need to constantly be asking two fundamental questions: What's happening now? and What's happening next?

The first question deals with intelligence gathering and the second deals with analysis. Even though your core beliefs and message are constant, the context for your ministry is changing rapidly. And it is your context that informs your strategy. That's why Paul, when explaining his philosophy of ministry in 1 Corinthians 9, said he was willing to become all things to all men in order to save some. (1 Corinthians 9:22) His strategy changed based on the context.

This is more important now than ever because we are no longer dealing with incremental change, but with what Robert Quinn describes as *deep change* in that it is both exponential and irreversible. If you are not paying attention, while you are micro-sleeping, the context for your ministry won't just pass you by, it will leap frog you altogether. And it's never coming back.

> *Robert Quinn's book,* Deep Change, *is a seminal text on change management. At the core of deep change is the recognition that we are dealing with something that is not incremental in scope and therefore will require a "bet the farm" risk to embrace it. Even if the change doesn't work, it is highly unlikely we will be able to go back to the old way. "Deep change differs from incremental change in that it requires new ways of thinking and behaving. It is…major in scope, discontinuous with the past and generally irreversible."[1] Deep change, therefore, does not follow the assumptions or models of ordinary, logical and rational planning.*
>
> *Deep changes thrusts leaders into the perfect storm of urgency, uncertainty and vulnerability. There is first a sense of urgency resulting from dissonance between the organization and its context. Leaders understand changes need to be made. What's happening now, in the world around us, is out of sync with our organization. Methods, systems and processes that once served us well are no longer effective.*
>
> *But the sense of urgency about the need for deep change does not answer the question, "what's next?" Deep change exposes the fallacy of thinking or feeling we are in control of our surroundings. This fuels a sense of uncertainty about what to change and insures whatever we do will expose us to great risk. This level of change goes beyond pilot projects and safe field tests.*
>
> *The combination of urgency and uncertainty only exacerbate the sense of vulnerability. We know we can't remain unchanged and thrive. We know incremental change is not the order of the day. But deep change plunges us into a state of increased vulnerability.*

---

[1] Robert Quinn, *Deep Change* (San Francisco: Jossey-Bass, 1996), 3

If you are an organizational leader in North American missions you know full well this is your world. Be encouraged. This combination of urgency, uncertainty and vulnerability creates an unprecedented window of opportunity for you to lead.

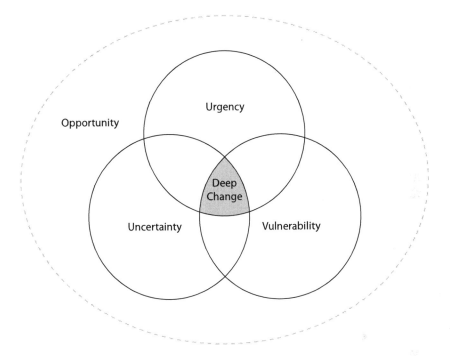

Something to think about, maybe even talk over with your team:

1. Read the Jack Welch quote for your team: "If the pace of change inside your organization is not greater than the pace of change outside your organization the end is near." On a scale of one to seven, with one being strongly disagree, and seven being strongly agree, what is your response to this statement? Why? Ask your team members to choose a response individually and then talk about your answers as a group.
2. What systems or processes does your organization have in place to insure the right people are wrestling with "what's happening now?" and "what's happening next?"
3. What aspects of your organization are, according to Robert Quinn's definition, experiencing deep change?

4. How are you insuring that your strategy is in sync with the ever-changing context in which you do ministry?

This content was originally posted as a Learning @ the Speed of Life vlog in September 2008.
To watch this vlog go to *www.TheMissionExchange.org/vlogArchives.php*

CHAPTER THREE
WHERE IS YOUR GREEN LINE

There is a lot of talk these days in the media and the church about the environment. All that has me thinking about what I describe as my "green line." By that I mean the line of activity or behavior that if someone crosses it I perceive them to be "out of bounds" as it relates to my conviction about being a good steward of creation. I believe everyone, even those who don't consider themselves to be environmentalists, has a green line. The question isn't do you have one, but where is it?

Indulge me with a little thought experiment. Imagine we are riding in your car and decide to get something to eat from a fast food restaurant. Let's say that I'm so hungry I finish my meal before we get to wherever we are driving and therefore neatly replace all of my trash in the paper bag the food first came in, roll down the window and throw the whole thing out on the ground. In most cases I will have crossed your green line, and not just because it's against the law to litter. Even if it were not illegal you would probably feel it is improper and I shouldn't do it. Even if you didn't know me very well you probably would be so frustrated with my behavior that you'd call me on it. At the very least, you would look aghast at my actions and it would have a negative effect on the tone of our conversation.

I had an interesting green line experience a number of years ago in China. I was travelling with a group of young adults on a very long train trip. Soon after boarding, we purchased "rice boxes," which were simply small Styrofoam boxes of rice, vegetables and some sort of not-so-readily-identifiable meat. (Then again, the chicken foot on top of the rice might be a giveaway.)

Having had previous experience both with traveling in China and eating rice boxes, I was enjoying mine but it was easy to tell that after only a few bites nearly all of my team members had decided it wasn't their ideal meal. The first student to look for a trash can found that it was only a very small plastic container hardly big enough to hold one rice box and therefore, after throwing his away, it was completely full.

Not long afterwards, a worker from the train came through our car, saw the waste basket was full, picked it up, dumped the rice box out the window, put the trash can back on the floor and left. After a moment of exchanging surprised looks between the students, another person put her rice box in the now empty can. The process we had just observed repeated itself: the attendant came through our car and the one rice box in the trash can was thrown out the window. One by one the remaining students took their turn discarding the unwanted meal.

What struck me about the whole situation was that while every one of us knew where the garbage would end up, no one could bring themselves to skip that more proper step in between and simply throw the rice box out the window. Doing so would have forced these students to cross their green line, just as it would for you if I were to throw my trash out of your car window.

Here's what I want you to think about. A growing number of Christ-followers, especially among the emerging generation, when thinking about getting involved with an organization, including your church or mission, are asking the question, "where is your green line?" And leaders or organizations that don't seem to care about consuming less or conserving more or reducing their carbon footprint may find themselves on the other side of the young leader's green line, just like I would be for you if I threw trash out your car window.

Please understand these people have not been brainwashed by environmental "whackos." Their beliefs about creation care have been shaped by a journey of spiritual formation as an extension of biblical discipleship. They can't conceive of an authentic and growing relationship with Jesus that doesn't somehow express itself with a concern for the environment. They are not likely to condemn you for being less concerned about this issue than they are, but an increasing number of them won't want to work for your organization or give to your ministry or volunteer for your projects if your green line is too far away from theirs.

The pragmatic bent in many leaders will prod them to say, "OK if we have to move our green line a little in order to be more next generation friendly then let's do it." I have a word of caution for you and it's really important that you hear me: there is a difference between a method and a value. If moving your green line is a method to attract a new group of people to your organization instead of a value that is being expressed in your organizational culture, your lack of authenticity will be obvious and you may be going backward instead of forward as it relates to building trust with the very people you want to attract.

So, I begin where we started with a simple question: Where is your green line? Should you consider, for all the right reasons, moving it? And just in case you are wondering when this all of a sudden become an issue anyway, my answer is, while you were micro-sleeping. If you aren't sure what I mean by that, you might want to revisit the previous chapter.

Something to think about, maybe even talk over with your team:

1. Think of a time when someone crossed your green line. What were the circumstances? How did you respond? What about the other person's behavior was offensive to you?
2. When was the last time you heard a message in a church or ministry context that challenged Christ-followers to engage in creation care? What can you remember about it?
3. If a young leader (or anyone, regardless of age) came and asked you what steps the church or mission in which you serve was taking to reduce your carbon footprint, what would you say? If they asked you if your church or mission viewed this as an issue that is important to God, what would you say?
4. A case could be made to support the idea that bad environmental stewardship disproportionately impacts the poorest of the poor. How might you seek to blend serving the poor in the name of Christ with creation care? Is this a worthy goal? Why or why not?

This content was originally posted as a Learning @ the Speed of Life vlog in October 2008.
To watch this vlog go to ***www.TheMissionExchange.org/vlogArchives.php***

For more information on this topic, consider this downloadable webinar in our online store at www.TheMissionExchange.org: *Small Footprint Big Handprint*, by Tri Robinson, based on his book by the same title.

CHAPTER FOUR
FROM INVENTION TO INNOVATION: HOW INNO-FRIENDLY IS YOUR ORGANIZATION?

I've never met an effective leader who wasn't on the lookout for the next big idea. Leaders intuitively understand the relationship between ideas and innovation and between innovation and increased effectiveness. It was Thomas Edison who said an idea is called *invention;* converting an idea into something useful for the customer and profitable for the company is called *innovation.* As a church or ministry leader, your bottom line is infinitely more important than any company, which is why innovation is just as important for you as any business leader.

One of my favorite stories from mission history that highlights the importance of innovation comes from the life of Hudson Taylor. As an emerging missionary in China, Hudson Taylor encountered several Chinese men who, as they went about their business, were continually looking up at him, talking amongst themselves and laughing. Curious and self-conscious, he soon approached the men and convinced them to tell him what they had found so amusing. He was dressed as was typical to Britain at the time and the men pointed out that his vest had a button on one side and a button hole on the other but clearly hadn't been made with enough material to actually close across his chest, which struck them as ridiculous.

It was at this moment that Taylor first realized he had cultural baggage which was creating a barrier for his evangelistic efforts. Mulling over this idea later convinced him to go to great lengths to remove those barriers, doing everything from abandoning his western dress to shaving nearly all of his head, as was typical for Chinese men, and dyeing what was left black. That was a paradigm busting innovation that continues to impact mission strategy and contextualized ministry today.

Hudson Taylor's experience not only illustrates innovation in mission, it raises two important questions: Where do you most need a fresh burst of innovation? How innovation friendly is your organizational culture?

Seth Godin, in his book *Free Prize Inside!*, makes a thought provoking statement: "There is no correlation between how good your idea is and how likely your organization will be to embrace it." We wrongly assume that if the right idea came along we would recognize it and implement it. History tells a different story. In fact, the more paradigm busting the idea, the greater the likelihood it will be resisted at first. This is why George Whitefield's innovative approach of preaching outdoors to common folk in Bristol was rejected at first, even by his friends. Few individuals see the potential in breakthrough ideas when they are first introduced and even fewer organizations are structured in a manner that readily turns invention into innovation.

While far from an exhaustive list, I want to highlight four limiting factors that affect the innovation-friendliness of your organizational culture:

1. *Elitist Mentality:* Research on the logic of diversity shows that a group of randomly selected individuals have a better chance of solving a complex problem than the same number of experts in that particular field. The experts will be much more homogeneous; they will likely have read the same books, trained in the same institutions and been collectively convinced about what won't work. They can't ask the dumb questions that often trigger new ideas.

Why is this important for you? Most churches and ministries limit key brainstorming sessions to insider experts, the "professional Christians" on their staff, unwittingly practicing a form of elitist thinking that will greatly reduce the "aha!" quotient of your meetings. I encourage you to randomly cycle people from every layer of your constituency through those key brainstorming sessions.

2. *Risk Averse Culture:* Speaking to a group of mission executives at one of our gatherings a few years ago, Cobie Langerak, President of Triaxia Partners, said, "Mediocrity has become a bigger problem for Christian leaders than failure." I agree. We are so convinced our constituents don't want to hear we tried something new that didn't work and we know how difficult it is to keep them from finding out so we repeatedly opt for safety over creativity resulting in mediocrity. Our problem is not that we are making too many mistakes. On the contrary, we are not making mistakes fast enough. When it comes to innovation, not making any mistakes is just as big of a problem as making the same ones over and over again.

3. *Bureaucratic Systems:* Here's an exercise for you: pick a box at random

in the bottom one third of your organizational chart and imagine this as the hypothetical epicenter of a breakthrough idea. (If your first thought was why the bottom third, reread my first point - you may be suffering from elitist thinking!) Now make a process chart showing how many meetings and approvals this idea would have to go through before it could be cleared for implementation along with a timeline showing how long it would take. You might be surprised at what you find. "Speed to market" is a phrase few ministry leaders would use in a brainstorming or planning session, but the fact of the matter is the rapid pace of change means the shelf life of your very best idea is constantly decreasing. Stability is not as important as agility when it comes to organizational development. The proverbial red tape is a powerful limiting factor many organizations need to address.

4. *Uni-directional Feedback:* Most innovation happens at the customer interface, the point of grassroots connection between your frontline staff and your constituents. Some time ago I was looking for a specific book for my Kindle on Amazon.com and when I saw that it wasn't available in an electronic version I had the thought that it would be nice to be able to email the publishers and tell them that I would have bought that book if it had been offered in the Kindle format. I sent a quick email to Amazon.com with that idea before exiting the website and quickly forgot about it. A few weeks later I was searching for another book which was also not available for the Kindle and, having the same thought occur to me, looked and realized that in just a matter of weeks they had created a link in the corner of the screen which read, "Tell the Publisher! I'd like to read this book on Kindle."

I may have been one of thousands of people who expressed the same idea and clearly someone took notice. But the problem is most churches and mission organizations have one-way communication corridors that flow from the top down. So the people with the power to embrace and execute new ideas rarely ever experience the operation of the ministry at the grassroots and have no consistent mechanism for getting feedback from the people who do. Senior pastors never pull in their own church parking lot one minute before the service is scheduled to start so they have no idea what people who do actually experience. Mission leaders rarely if ever experience the activities of their mission outside of padded walls of preference that come with the status of being CEO.

Something to think about, maybe even talk over with your team:

1. What is the most innovative step your church or mission has taken in the last year? Where did the idea originate? How long did it take to go from ideation to implementation? What does all this reveal about the inno-friendliness of your organization?
2. Review the first limiting factor, elitist thinking. How proactive is your organization with regard to embracing the logic of diversity and widening the circles of conversation when it comes to planning?
3. It has often been said that the church is ten to twenty years behind culture when it comes to embracing technology or leading change. What evidence would you provide from the life of your organization that you are ahead of the curve?
4. Describe the bottom up feedback loops you have in place that keep you in touch with the "customer interface." How efficient are these systems? What was the last piece of data you received from these systems that drove innovation?

This content was originally posted as a Learning @ the Speed of Life vlog in November 2008.
To watch this vlog go to *www.TheMissionExchange.org/vlogArchives.php*

CHAPTER FIVE
WHY COMPETITION (EVEN IN MINISTRY) IS UNAVOIDABLE AND WHAT TO DO ABOUT IT

You probably have heard the story about the guy who gets rescued from a desert island and when the crew from the ship arrives they discover one hut where the man lived and two other huts with crosses on the top on either side of the small island. They asked the man about the two huts and he explains that one of them is where he went to church, where he worshiped and prayed while waiting to be rescued. The obvious follow-up question is "What about the other hut with the cross on top?" to which the man responded, "That's the church I used to go to."

Crazy as it sounds, I believe competition in ministry is inevitable; the question isn't how do we remove it but rather how do we respond to it? I realize you are already pushing back on that thought so give me just a minute to clarify my position. Church and ministry leaders wrongly assume that competition is merely a selfish motive or negative attitude behind the desire for increased market share, to grow my ministry at the expense of someone else.

I believe that is an incomplete picture. I want to suggest competition is rooted not only in the heart or mind of a leader but also in the options and decisions of the customer. It is a market reality that exists whenever the customer has a choice between similar options. In political terms, we describe a competitive election as one in which there are more people on the ballot than offices to be filled; that's what makes it competitive.

What I want you to see is that your commitment to kingdom thinking and practice of partnership principles does not change the fact your prospective constituents, whether they are donors, volunteers, staff or parishioners, have to choose between your ministry and some other similar opportunity. So when I say competition is unavoidable what I really mean is in order for your prospective constituents to get involved in your church or ministry they will have to choose between similar options competing for their attention. You can't make that go away. Nor should you try.

So what do we do about it? How should we respond to this "competitive" reality? I want to give three simple suggestions about how to respond to your "competition."

1. *Speak positively about them.* We may question or even challenge some aspects of how others do ministry in private, but publically we should commit to speak positively about them. I had a friend in college named Jean who was committed to always speaking and thinking positively about others. I remember one day after leaving chapel there was a sort of unanimous but silent understanding that it had been the worst chapel message of our college career.

Because everyone knew Jean for his optimistic, kingdom-minded perspective, several people specifically asked him what he thought of the lesson, wondering what possible good thing he could have to say. He paused for a moment and then told us, "I'm sure God can use it."

I understand that the phrase sounds trite, but for some reason it stuck with me and through all these years whenever I am tempted to criticize the motives or methods of another leader, ministry, organization, or church, that thought still rings in my mind: I'm sure God can use it.

In Philippians 1:15-18, Paul admits that some preach the gospel out of envy and rivalry, even selfish ambition. He goes on to say the important thing is that, whether from false motives or true, Christ is preached. Though I might not agree with everything happening in another church or ministry, I rejoice in the fact that Christ is preached and therefore commit to speak positively about them.

2. *Share generously with them.* Because I'm not worried about increasing my own market share or finding a competitive advantage, I am free to share everything I'm learning with others. So whether it's more efficient systems or effective methods or valuable experience, freely I have received, freely I give. That doesn't mean we can't provide services to other ministries that involve fair and reasonable fees. It does mean we don't withhold anything we are learning that could enable another ministry to reap a greater harvest.

3. *Serve passionately alongside them.* Because we share the same ultimate bottom line with other churches or ministries we are free to partner with them in actual frontline ministry. It is easier to speak positively about others and share generously with others than it is to serve passionately alongside them.

My friend Marv Newell, Executive Director of CrossGlobal Link, reminded me recently that while Solomon said two are better than one, he didn't say two were easier than one. Here's a question we need to be asking again and again as we plan our ministry initiatives: Who could we partner with to expand the reach and increase the impact of this project?

Competition in ministry is unavoidable, at least as it relates to the fact our prospective constituents have to choose between more than one ministry opportunity. The motive for seeking to engage a wider constituency is not to increase market share but to advance the kingdom.

Pursue your ministry with excellence. Offer your very best and raise the bar for others knowing you are committed to speak positively, share generously and serve passionately.

If you are "competing" with several other organizations for a grant from a foundation, it would be ridiculous to intentionally decide not to make the most compelling case you can, justifying your poor presentation as an act of kingdom-minded generosity that might open the door for one of the other groups to get the money.

An important principle of business is differentiation. Companies seek to differentiate themselves from their competitors in hopes of gaining an advantage with customers. Clearly this focus on market share is not something ministry leaders should emulate. But the principle of differentiation is important for another reason.

Competition exists, even in ministry, because we do not operate in a monopoly. As long as prospective constituents have a choice about what church they will attend or which mission organization they will engage, competition is in place. That's true regardless of how kingdom-minded the leaders of these organizations might be.

You need to do the hard work of organizational self-awareness (who are we and where are we going?) that leads to differentiation not so you can gain an advantage over other ministries but so you can make it easier for prospective constituents to determine if they are a good fit with your organization. In this way you are serving prospective constituents and modeling for other similar organizations how they can increase their own effectiveness.

> *Leaders who can clearly articulate vision will do a great service for followers, present and future. Unfortunately the skills associated with refining a clear vision and communicating it effectively are either not taught at all or not given proper emphasis in many of the institutions primarily charged with the responsibility to train church and mission leaders. Just being able to "raise the vision flag up the flagpole" will in itself differentiate a leader from many others who are more concerned about accommodating every passing fancy in an attempt to satisfy the wants and preferences of the widest possible constituency. It never works.*

Something to think about, maybe even talk over with your team:

1. How difficult is it for you to separate the idea of competition from a motive in the heart of a leader to a market reality stemming from choices that need to be made by customers/constituents?
2. Mentally audit your conversations about "the competition" over the last ninety days. How would your "competition" rank you in terms of speaking positively?
3. What is the best evidence of your commitment to "share generously" in the last year?
4. Ask three to five leaders in your organization to share how they would differentiate your ministry from "the competition." To what extent is your vision/mission message clear, aligned and well positioned to differentiate you from others?

This content was originally posted as a Learning @ the Speed of Life vlog in November 2008.
To watch this vlog go to ***www.TheMissionExchange.org/vlogArchives.php***

For more information on this topic, consider the downloadable webinars in our online store at www.TheMissionExchange.org: *Three Rails of Partnership* by Ellen Livingood, *Authentic Inter-Cultural Partnerships* by Daniel Rickett, and *Partner Friendly Organizations* by Brian O'Connell.

CHAPTER SIX
THE "PUNKIFICATION" OF MISSIONS

A recent ideological shift worth taking a look at is something I refer to as the "punkification" of missions. I realize that may require a little explanation, so for those of you who weren't alive or can't remember the 70's, let me give you a quick history lesson on punk music. Punk rock was known for short, edgy songs with stripped down instrumentation and anti-establishment lyrics. At the heart of punk culture was a do-it-yourself philosophy that intentionally blurred the lines between the audience and the musician. One of punk music's classic advertisements says it all with a diagram showing three finger positions on the neck of a guitar with the caption: "Here's one chord, here's two more, now form your own band."

Punk rockers typically emerged from garages, producing and distributing their own records. That seems mainstream now, but remember, we are talking about the early to mid 1970's before there was such ready access to all of the necessary equipment for this to be done at home. The simple message of punk music is this: everyone gets to play; go ahead, form your own band.

What does all this have to do with missions? I think you probably get it by now. We are riding the final wave of the punkification of missions and the message is pretty much the same: everyone gets to play.

In his book, *The World is Flat,* Thomas Friedman popularized what happens when you combine the combustible mixture of do it yourself punk philosophy with technology that is faster, smaller and cheaper: globalization. I want to highlight two aspects of globalization that are driving the punkification of missions: *the democratization of information* and the *decentralization of initiative.*

First, let's look at the democratization of information. When information is widely accessible and readily available it ceases to become valuable as a source of power. And information has never been so readily available in real time.

Let me give you two personal examples. Last fall I attended a powerful talk by Thom Wolf. His lesson was sincerely challenging to me so when he referenced a certain article I pulled out my PDA and looked up the article online where I quickly discovered an entire book that had been written to expand upon the ideas in the article. I went to Amazon.com, found and ordered the book, and less than two minutes after hearing of the existence of an article written ten years earlier, I'd received a confirmation message from Amazon.com telling me that the book which expanded on this material had already been shipped. It was waiting for me when I got home a few days later.

Only six months afterwards I was participating in one of the webinars our organization sponsors when the speaker quoted a book that really interested me. Not long before this I had invested in an Amazon Kindle which I had with me and in less than 90 seconds after hearing of the book I was reading a downloaded sample of it. (If you are a speaker, be aware that an increasing number of your listeners are fact-checking your illustrations and statistics while you are still talking.)

One of the powerful ramifications of the punkification of missions is your constituents are no longer dependent on you for information; they can get it from 100 other sources, many of them non-professionals. When we think about technology leveling the playing field we normally focus on downloadable content. But that is very short-sighted. *Uploading is the most revolutionary form of collaboration in the world.* Everyone with a cell phone is now an ad hoc reporter for CNN using text messages, pictures and videos to relay breaking news stories. Here's one pic, here's two more, now write your own blog.

What does all this mean for church and mission leaders? Far too many mission organizations are operating with a download paradigm in an upload world. Listen to what media mogul Rupert Murdoch said in a 2006 speech:

"Societies or companies (I would add churches or mission organizations) that expect a glorious past to shield them from the forces of change driven by advancing technology will fail and fall. Power is moving away from the old elite in our industries, the editors, the chief executives, and let's face it, the proprietors. A new generation of media consumers has risen demanding content delivered when they want it, how they want it, and very much as they want it."[1]

The main idea I want you to catch here is the forces of change driven by advancing technology don't really care about your glorious past and power is shifting away from the old elite.

The second issue fueling the punkification of missions is *the decentralization of initiative.* This is what punk philosophy is all about, do-it-yourself. Empowered by a steady stream of information and the technology needed to go global ten minutes after plugging in a computer, everyone with an idea is

---

[1] Matt Mason, *The Pirate's Dilemma* (New York, NY: FREE PRESS, 2008), location 808, Kindle edition

ready to change the world.

Kevin Kelly, senior maverick at *Wired* magazine said in his article, *"We are the Web"*:

"It is not impossible to imagine that one day everyone alive will (on average) write a song, author a book, make a video, craft a weblog, and code a program… What happens when the data flow is asymmetrical but in favor of the creators? It was long assumed that producing any product of substance or complexity takes some kind of hierarchical organization or institution. The assumption was that you needed top-down vertical integration to get such things done. But thanks to the newfound ability to upload you can now produce really complex things, as an individual or as part of a community, with much less hierarchy and much less money than ever before."[2]

Individuals and churches alike are embracing a punk missions philosophy; now that information has been democratized and initiative has been decentralized the power-brokers of the old school are discovering they are no longer in control. Get used to it; we live in an upload world.

All of this can be very unsettling, especially if you are used to calling the shots and being in the seat of power. Sure there are challenges associated with the punkification of missions. But it's a lot easier to steer a moving vehicle than a parked one. There's a Chinese proverb that says: "When the winds of change are blowing, some people build shelters and others build windmills."

If we don't figure out how to collaborate creatively--if we use all of our metaphorical bandwidth for downloading--our constituents will increasingly pursue "punk missions" that circumvent entirely the old school structures. Perhaps they will rewrite the punk music add: here's a cell phone, here's a computer, now launch your own mission.

Something to think about, maybe even talk over with your team:

1. How has your organization already been impacted by the "punkification" of missions? How have you (and other leaders) reacted?
2. How has the lack of control of the flow of information limited your organizational power-base? How is the democratization of information affecting your relationship with your constituents?

---

[2] Kevin Kelly, *Wired* - www.wired.com/wired/archive/13.08/tech.html

3. What is the most positive example of the decentralization of initiative you have encountered as an organization? How could you seek to replicate that in the future?
4. What is the most negative example of the decentralization of initiative you have encountered as an organization? How could you seek to improve that in the future?
5. Are you building shelters or windmills? Are you still operating with a download paradigm in an upload world? To what extent are you making space for co-collaboration with the grassroots of your constituency?

This content was originally posted as a Learning @ the Speed of Life vlog in March 2009.
To watch this vlog go to *www.TheMissionExchange.org/vlogArchives.php*

DEEPER
If you want to explore this idea further I recommend Matt Mason's book, *The Pirate's Dilemma, How Youth Culture is Reinventing Capitalism*. This is a brash, in your face reality check drawing heavily from illustrations and observations from popular culture.

CHAPTER SEVEN
THE POWER
OF VIRAL MINISTRY

In the previous chapter I introduced you to the punkification of missions and highlighted the fact that we live in a world where everyone gets to be a content creator. The flow of data has become asymmetrical--more is going up than coming down. If you insist on operating with a download paradigm in an upload world you are going to marginalize yourself as a leader and render your organization irrelevant.

You might be thinking the punkification of missions sounds a lot like what others have described as the "amaturization" of missions. I say yes and no. The amaturization of missions shines the spotlight exclusively on the downside of living in an upload world. The decentralization of initiative has resulted in un-professional missionaries chasing around the world in uncoordinated ministries. Many of these initiatives create more problems than they solve no matter how good it makes us feel to be involved.

But there is an upside to living in an upload world and I want to highlight one piece of it: viral ministry. To my surprise some of my more progressive and innovative mission leader friends didn't know what the term viral means so let me begin with an explanation. Viral marketing uses pre-existing social networks to communicate a message or enhance a brand, often leveraged by technology through digital pictures, videos, email or even text messages. It is word of mouth on techno-steroids.

Very few church and mission leaders have figured out how to operate with an upload paradigm, which explains why we have yet to fully tap in to the power of viral ministry. Matt Mason, in his book *The Pirate's Dilemma,* makes this statement: "Punk made it very clear that we could do everything ourselves, and purpose should be at least as important as profit."[1] For something to "go viral" it has to have a purpose that goes beyond making a profit. That plays right in to our hands.

Sometimes the purpose of a viral message is frivolous, other times it is mali-

---

[1] Matt Mason, *The Pirate's Dilemma* (New York, NY: FREE PRESS, 2008), location 3572, Kindle edition

cious. But the purpose in a viral message can also be significant. Filipinos have used text messaging to effectively stage massive political demonstrations. The Obama campaign leveraged viral messages to mobilize young voters. What does this look like in a church or mission context?

I'd like to give you an example of an organization jump starting viral ministry from the life of 12Stone church, where I attend here in metro Atlanta. In the fall of 2008 our senior pastor felt prompted to find a way for our church to intentionally act in extravagant generosity in spite of the reflexive desire to hoard our assets in light of the weakening economy. As a result of that initiative, from Thanksgiving to the end of 2008, a campaign was launched called "Intentional Acts of Christmas" in which the church freed up $250,000 in $100 increments to be distributed to individuals or family units from the congregation who agreed to sign a covenant stating that they would use the money to bless someone else.

The response was so enthusiastic that the total amount of seed money from the church was adjusted upward to $300,000 so that everyone who wanted a chance to participate would be able to do so. We were also challenged to use additional personal funds, along with the seed money from the church, to expand the impact of this outreach initiative. The personal contributions to the cause totaled nearly $400,000, bringing the total invested in our community to nearly $700,000.

This example of viral ministry reinforces four principles of viral marketing, which I have slightly modified from Matt Mason's book, *The Pirate's Dilemma:*

1. *Give your audience as many options as guidelines.* 12Stone asked people to sign a covenant to say they would use the funds to bless others but then provided lots of options about how to go about it. The church offered support in selecting a worthy cause but did not control the decision. But what if someone took the money and used it on themselves? That was a necessary risk the church was prepared to take in order to get many others to "upload."

2. *Avoid the limelight.* Remember the cause has to take precedence over "profit." The web site 12Stone created to enable people to share stories and connect with needs was virtually anonymous. Participants were told this is not about promoting a church. The cause was always front and center.

3. *Feed the virus according to its size.* When it is hungry feed it; when it's not don't force it. Forcing the message would be guerilla marketing not viral marketing. 12Stone started out with $250K and bumped it up to $300K in response to the number of people who wanted in. The virus was hungry so we fed it.

4. *Remember, viruses have a short life span.* Viral marketing initiatives won't last forever. We started at Thanksgiving and closed down Intentional Acts of Christmas officially the end of December. But the spirit of the campaign reinforced a larger value for giving ourselves away, which is what this was about in the first place.

One final example. As a seventh grader Zach Hunter started the Loose Change to Loosen Chains movement. At the time of this writing Zach is seventeen and considers himself a modern day abolitionist, driven by a passion to end slavery and human trafficking.

In a download world where everything is hierarchical and you need an organization with vertical integration in order to produce meaningful results, people like Zach have only two choices: stand on the sidelines and watch, or hitch their wagon to someone else's caravan. But in an upload world that has viral capacity you can create a movement without brick and mortar or by-laws or a board of directors. And that is what Zach has done. Just Google Loose Change to Loosen Chains and see for yourself.

One of the positive by-products of the punkification of missions is viral ministry and it has the potential to spread like, well a pandemic. Only in an upload world can you engage, or could we say "infect," hundreds of thousands of people in a matter of days for free. By leveraging twitter, youtube, facebook and other social networking sites it is possible to communicate and mobilize large groups without traditional systems or structures. That's what makes it so scary. That's what makes it so powerful.

> *One of the interesting elements of Zach Hunter's viral initiative, Loose Change to Loosen Chains, is that the grassroots movement has spawned hybrid partnerships with formal organizations. Zach has connected with Gary Haugen's International Justice Mission (IJM), which helps promote the initiative as part of their ministry to youth and children. IJM doesn't own Loose Change but there is a common passion and shared value system that opens the door for a viral initiative to benefit from organizational systems. We need more of this kind of collaboration but it won't happen if we are afraid to embrace and unleash the virus!*

Something to think about, maybe even talk over with your team:

1. I've highlighted viral ministry as the upside of living in an upload world. What other "ups" can you see in this new reality? To what extent is your organization leveraging these for kingdom good?
2. Review the paragraph about viral marketing. When was the last time you were engaged with or the recipient of something that "went viral?" How could this experience serve as a laboratory for viral initiatives connected with your organization?
3. Review the four rules of viral marketing. Which of these is most difficult for you to employ? Why? How will you overcome this limiting factor?
4. Viral ministry as I've highlighted it here results from a creative combination of an organization that primes the pump (like 12Stone Church did to get things started) or one that creates a hybrid partnership with a viral initiative (like Zach Hunter did with Loose Change). Which of these options best suits your situation? What would need to happen in your organization to do both?

This content was originally posted as a Learning @ the Speed of Life vlog in April 2009.
To watch this vlog go to *www.TheMissionExchange.org/vlogArchives.php*

If you want to explore this idea further I recommend Matt Mason's book, *The Pirate's Dilemma, How Youth Culture is Reinventing Capitalism*. This is a brash, in your face reality check drawing heavily from illustrations and observations from popular culture. I also recommend Seth Godin's book, *Tribes, We Need You to Lead Us*.

CHAPTER EIGHT
WHO'S YOUR CDO? WHY EVERY SUCCESSFUL ENTERPRISE NEEDS A CHIEF DESTRUCTION OFFICER

Success always brings its own set of challenges. Positive change, and that's what success is, never eliminates problems. It merely enables us to trade our current problems for a new set of challenges we have come to believe are preferable. If you are a local church leader and you plan a special Sunday, get your people to invite their friends, and expose more people to the gospel than you ever have before on a single day, we would all categorize that as a huge success. But if the crowd was fourty percent larger than your parking lot and you didn't make plans to deal with the extra traffic, this awesome success would come with its own set of problems. To use a football metaphor, you out-kicked your coverage. It has a downside, but it's better than getting the punt blocked.

You may remember the UPS commercial from the late 90's that showed two guys sitting in front of a computer as they were getting ready to launch their new web site. They took the site live and then started watching the orders come flying in. Their high fives soon turned into "oh no's!" when it dawned on them they did not have the capacity to fulfill the number of orders their web site was generating. It wasn't a very realistic commercial but it got the point across.

All things being equal, I'm sure you would agree with me that when given the choice, you'd take the problems that come with a successful organization over those accompanying an organization in decline any day. One of the high level skills of managing change is the ability to predict and prepare for unintended consequences. But just because some consequences of change are unintentional does not mean they are unpredictable.

I want to pull back to the 50K foot level and explore some critical and yet predictable consequences of successful enterprises. These dynamics apply to individual organizations but I want to apply them to the missions enterprise in general as opposed to an organization in particular.

The North American mission movement has experienced unprecedented success. Quoting from my colleague, Paul McKaughan, in his article, *Deleveraging Markets and Missions[1]*, the North American mission enterprise has "enjoyed a protracted and unparalleled period of economic and organizational growth… our mission community is far wealthier, better educated and more comfortably sustained than ever in history." Paul goes on to explain why deleveraging is in order; I want to build on his ideas.

Success almost always translates into growth. I realize some prefer the idea of health but I'm including that as a form of growth. Two fundamental, albeit unintended, consequences of sustained growth are a *decrease in urgency* and an *increase in complexity*. I'm not saying it is impossible to sustain urgency for continued growth when you are in a season of expansion but I am saying to do so will require energy and intentionality. But there is nothing you can do to change the fact that sustained growth brings increased complexity.

Think of it like this: If your mission grows from 100 missionaries in twenty countries to 500 missionaries in fifty countries the expanded scope will produce increased complexity. The same is true for a church going from 250 to 1,000 in average attendance. If you don't deal with the challenges of increased complexity you will not be able to sustain your growth. In this situation, quite naturally, urgency tends to shift away from producing new growth toward solving the problems of increased complexity that came with the growth you have already experienced. That is understandable and appropriate, for a season.

Increased complexity calls for more and better policies as well as refined systems and structures. Here's the problem. The unintended consequences of dealing with increased complexity are first, professionalism, and second, elitism. (Remember I'm applying this to the entire missions enterprise not one organization.) As organizations learn to deal with increased complexity they produce experts who refine their discipline. Eventually educational institutions recruit these experts to become professors and they start offering new specialized classes and even degrees.

For example, in the missions enterprise we have various categories of experts in a wide variety of fields ranging from church planting to member care to ethnomusicology, and the list could go on. A similar kind of list could be generated with consultants serving the local church. Please don't misunderstand me; I'm

---

[1] Available from www.TheMissionExchange.org via our online store.

not saying we don't need these experts or that they don't have anything important to contribute. They do.

So what am I saying? Over time professionalism brings with it a measure of elitism.

By elitism I don't mean a look down your nose snobbery, at least it doesn't have to be that way. What I mean by elitism is a deepening commitment to what we know as experts, which fuels risk aversion and a diminished openness to new ideas that do not surface from inside the professional community. (Remember the lessons from the publishing world in chapter 1?)

Listen to what Kevin Kelly, senior maverick at *Wired* magazine says in his book *New Rules for the New Economy:*

"The problem with the top is not too much perfection but too little perspective. Great success...tends to block a longer, larger view of the opportunities available... and of the rapidly shifting terrain ahead...Not every success needs to be abandoned drastically, but every success needs to be questioned drastically."[2]

Economist Joseph Schumpteter calls the progressive act of destroying success "creative destruction."[3] Management guru Tom Peters suggests that the skills associated with creating success and destroying success are diametrically opposed to each other and cannot be done by the same person. Peters goes on to say that in this rapidly changing environment every company needs a Chief Destruction Officer.[4]

I believe this is right where we find ourselves in the North American mission enterprise. The unintended consequences of success have brought a decrease of urgency as well as an increase of complexity. Urgency has not diminished as it relates to the Great Commission, but rather in terms of great innovation. Having been forced to respond to the increased complexity that comes with the growth of the mission enterprise has birthed both professionalism and elitism.

We are in need of a new breed of leaders, the Chief Destruction Officers. Here's my proposed job description:

1. *Wreak havoc on the status quo with relentless urgency.* Just because something is working now doesn't mean it will work tomorrow. We simply can't afford to wait for a strategy or methodology to stop working before we find a better way. Remember, all success should be questioned drastically.

2. *Rail against incrementalism.* Nicholas Negroponte, director of the MIT media lab, says, "Incrementalism is innovation's worst enemy." CDO's need to be

---

[2] Kevin Kelly, *New Rules for the New Economy* (New York, NY: Viking) 1998
[3] Ibid, 86
[4] Ibid, 86

prepared to embrace deep change and encourage paradigm pioneers. So much of what Christian leaders purport as innovation is merely tweaking "what is" instead of creating "what's next."

3. *Focus on the fringes where flexibility and organizational dexterity are in greater supply and there is less resistance to change.* Be prepared to look outside the circles of expert opinion beyond the insider professionals for new ideas. (See chapter four, From Invention to Innovation.)

4. *Spawn new structures.* When you find something that works on the fringes resist the temptation to pull it toward the center of your organizational identity or you will likely kill it. Instead, consider spawning a new structure that relates in some creative way to your organization so as to give the innovation time to stand on its own.

Much more could be said about this and my goal here is really just to get the conversation started. More than lots of answers I want to come back to a single question I posed in the title of this chapter: Who's your CDO, - chief destruction officer? I believe every successful enterprise needs one, including yours.

Something to think about, maybe even talk over with your team:

1. Think of a recent success story in your organization, something that worked out even better than you expected. What were the unintended consequences of success and how did you deal with them?
2. Where have you experienced sustained success and how are you doing when it comes to resisting the tendency to have a decrease in urgency? How has the complexity that is always the byproduct of sustained success contributed to complacency when it comes to continued growth?
3. What examples would you cite in your organization of "creative destruction?"
4. Review the four suggestions presented as the core job description of a Chief Destruction Officer. Who in your organization is best suited to perform these functions? How counter cultural are these activities?

This content was originally posted as a Learning @ the Speed of Life vlog in May 2009.
To watch this vlog go to *www.TheMissionExchange.org/vlogArchives.php*

Question:

What do you get when you combine

36 **book summaries**
electronically delivered, 3 per month

24 **live webinars**
average 2 per month

12 **author interviews**
MP3 downloads, 1 per month

6 **global issues updates**
bi-monthly downloadable webinar

3 **and 3 live conferences?**

1

Answer:

1 year of member benefits in The Mission Exchange

See all the categories of membership and a full explanation of our member benefits on the following two pages.

New categories of membership include individual, church and educational affiliate beginning at $99 per year.

Connect with The Mission Exchange

THE MISSION EXCHANGE
Empowering the Global Mission Community

❭ Getting Connected

Getting connected with The Mission Exchange will open a door of shared learning, mutual accountability and trusted partnership with other like-minded evangelical mission leaders. We offer an innovative combination of online resources and live training events designed to add value to mission leaders and stimulate partnership.

The grid on the next page displays the categories of relationship with The Mission Exchange along with corresponding Member Benefits.

To qualify as a **MEMBER** your organization must be a registered charity in the US or Canada, have at least $100,000 of annual revenue, agree with the National Association of Evangelicals statement of faith and be involved in cross cultural mission by sending missionaries or offering support service to the Great Commission community.

To qualify as an **ASSOCIATE MEMBER** your organization must be a member in good standing of another mission association that has been approved by The Mission Exchange board of directors. (Currently the only association so approved is CrossGlobal Link.)

We ask **AFFILIATES** to agree with the National Association of Evangelicals statement of faith as well as to affirm the vision, mission and core values of The Mission Exchange. There are three categories of Affiliate Membership:
  · **Individual Affiliate**   - $99 per person
  · **Church Affiliate**   - $279 for church wide staff and leadership
  · **Educational Affiliate** - $379 for all Professors, Staff and Students of a
                    Seminary, College, University or training program
                    (such as DTS, etc.).

Note: Affiliate memberships are available in our online store and are prorated based on the date purchased.

We encourage you to consider connecting with The Mission Exchange as outlined above but it is still possible to participate in training, networking events and live webinars as a non-member. If you have any questions, feel free to contact us at Connect@TheMissionExchange.org.

Membership Options

	Training & Networking Events	Live Webinars	Downloadable Webinars	Global Issues Updates	Professional Service Network	Leader's Edge Book Summary	improve Organizational Development Process (see page 71)	Credentialing Relationship
Member	Yes 20% discount	Yes Free	Yes $9.95ea	Yes Free	Yes 5-25% discount	Yes Free	Yes 50% discount	Yes – use of Member seal
Associate Member	Yes 15% discount	Yes Free	Yes $19.95ea	Yes Free	Yes 5-25% discount	Yes Free	Yes 20% discount	Yes – use of Associate Member seal
Affiliate Member | Individual · Church · Educational	Yes 10% discount	Yes $9.95ea	Yes $19.95ea	Yes Free	No	Yes Free	Yes 10% discount	No
Non Member	Limited Access	Yes $39.95ea	Yes $29.95ea	Yes $19.95ea	No	No	Yes No discount	No

For detailed information about these member benefits download the PDF version of EXCHANGE magazine from www.TheMissionExchange.org.

What others mission leaders are saying about **The Mission Exchange**

"I'm very encouraged by the forward momentum and effective resources offered by The Mission Exchange. We've utilized the webinars to increase our understanding around key areas. We continue to benefit from these value-added services."

~ Andrea Buczynski
Vice President, Global Leadership Development, Campus Crusade for Christ.

"I'm impressed how The Mission Exchange has consistently and successfully engaged those of us as mission leaders in fresh thinking and stimulating dialogue on so many key topics relevant to our ministries today."

~ Jon Lewis
President & CEO, Partners International

"The Mission Exchange has provided numerous opportunities for our agency leadership to have a seat at the table with other evangelical mission leaders. The webinars have proven to be excellent avenues to dialogue with various experts about the challenges facing mission endeavors in this new century."

~ James F. Forlines
General Director, Free Will Baptist International Missions

"It is an encouragement to be part of The Mission Exchange and know God has raised up so many organizations devoted to fulfilling the Great Commission. The diversity of size and focus of member entities enhance the value of networking and partnership in seeking to carry out our mission."

~ Jerry Rankin
President, International Mission Board, SBC

"I know from personal experience The Mission Exchange is adding value to mission organizations and I'm excited about their commitment to expand these quality services to local churches."

~ Rob Bugh
Senior Pastor, Wheaton Bible Church

CHAPTER NINE
HOW THE NEXT GENERATION IS REDEFINING LOYALTY AND WHY IT CHANGES EVERYTHING

If I were to ask you to make a list of the most important leadership issues impacting the context of ministry today I'm not sure loyalty would be in your top five. In fact some might even suggest loyalty may be an important topic but question if it is a leadership issue at all.

I believe the subject of loyalty, as it relates to leadership, is especially important today because we are in a transition window between two paradigms, two ways of understanding loyalty, largely across a generational divide. In fact the transition has already happened, in spite of the fact many leaders have yet to fully notice it or understand it.

In general, senior leaders tend to operate from what I call an Institutional Paradigm of loyalty, which flows from a shared history, ideology (in a church or ministry context we could say theology) and polity. If your spiritual heritage flows from a certain tradition there is an expectation that your shared history and theology should produce loyalty, which is measured primarily by how much you support the hallmark programs and projects of the institution.

Thirty years ago if a family moved from one part of the country to another, when it came to finding a church home, the question wasn't what kind of church are we going to attend, it was which church from our denomination are we going to attend. And of course if there wasn't a church with which we shared a history, we would certainly limit our search to one that shared the distinctive of our theology. People would offer a disclaimer saying, "There was no Wesleyan church in our community so we landed in a Nazarene church." Of course it could just as easily have been a Free Methodist church or whatever was closest to their theology.

If you felt called to ministry or to the mission field there was really no consideration about who your ordaining body would be or who your sending organization would be. Institutional Loyalty ruled the day.

There are two key words for Institutional Loyalty: exclusivity and entitlement. By exclusivity I mean a focus on our uniqueness, our distinctive in terms of theology or polity, what makes us different from others. By entitlement I'm not referring to the traditional understanding where grassroots individuals feel they are entitled to services from an institution. On the contrary, it is where institutions feel entitled to loyalty from their constituents.

The second paradigm of loyalty, which has surfaced with the emergence of the next generation of leaders, is what I call the Relational Paradigm. While the Institutional Paradigm flows from a shared history, ideology and polity, the Relational Paradigm flows from shared identity, the presence of capacity and windows of opportunity. A shared identity does not require a common history. If a person identifies with your vision, with the direction and calling or cause about which you are passionate and if this person believes you have a measure of capacity and provide windows of opportunity to engage her giftedness to make a difference, she can be fiercely loyal.

The key words in the Institutional Paradigm are exclusivity and entitlement; the key words in the Relational Paradigm of loyalty are diversity and engagement. By diversity I mean a willingness to engage with more than one organization even when they don't have a shared history, where there are differences in theology and polity. By engagement I mean recognition that we must add value in order to instill loyalty; it cannot be taken for granted.

Please understand, I'm not suggesting that no one serving in an Institution ever had a vision or a sense of calling, a measure of capacity or attempted to create space for others to engage. What I am saying is the perspective of the Institutional Paradigm is that loyalty can be and should be expected because of shared history, ideology and polity even when a sense of identity, capacity and opportunity around a common vision doesn't exist.

You may not like this seismic shift in the redefinition of loyalty but you can't afford to pretend it hasn't happened or that somehow you are going to put things back the way they were. Those days are gone forever.

This has powerful ramifications for church and mission leaders. If you are serving in a denominational context you have to have noticed this change already. But mission leaders serving in a cross-denominational context are not insulated from this loyalty paradigm shift. A lot could be said about this but I want to highlight three new realities that flow from the relational paradigm of loyalty.

1. *It is re-defining the meaning of career.* In the relational paradigm it is not disloyal to sign up with a mission (or any organization really) and serve for two to three years and then move on to something else. Young leaders expect to get experience in multiple career fields; to them it is normal not unstable. They have a much more holistic understanding of being on mission and don't believe the only way to be faithful to "the call" is to serve in "full time ministry." I realize this may challenge some of your traditions, wreak havoc with your structures and complicate your long-term plans. (That's why you need a Chief Destruction Officer.)

2. *It is limiting the number of theological hills they are willing to die on.* The Institutional Paradigm is marked by exclusivity, a sense of pride in what makes us unique, our distinctive, especially as it relates to our doctrine and theology. But young leaders operating from a relational paradigm struggle to accept the argument that we have to open a work in a particular village in spite of the fact there are several other teams there because there isn't one of "our kind of churches" in the area. I'm not talking about compromise on the core essentials of the gospel. I'm not saying you should abandon your theological distinctive. What I am saying is young leaders operating from a relational paradigm are much more open to working with a diversity of others even if they don't share our unique theological distinctive. Frankly, I find this aspect of the relational paradigm refreshing.

3. *It is pressing centralized authority structures to move from controlling to empowering.* Church and mission leaders who spend their leadership capital policing the uniqueness of their theology and the technicalities of compliance with their systems and structures and measure loyalty by how readily followers get in step with a top down agenda are in for a very difficult journey. I challenge you to repurpose your institution or organization around a value-added, service-oriented commitment to empowerment that is compatible with a relational paradigm.

Please hear me, the question isn't if this change will happen. It has already taken place. The most loyal step you can take is to get busy reorienting your philosophy of leadership and organizational culture.

2 Paradigms of Loyalty

Institutional Paradigm	Relational Paradigm
Shared history	Shared identity
Shared ideology/theology	Presence of capacity
Shared polity	Sense of opportunity
Key Words: exclusivity & entitlement	Key Words: diversity & engagement

Something to think about, maybe even talk over with your team:

1. What is the dominant paradigm of loyalty held by the senior leaders of your organization? What specific evidence would you offer to support your answer?
2. How does your organization fight against (or need to fight against) an entitlement mindset, believing your constituents should "get with the program" regardless of the perceived value added?
3. Consider inviting a group of younger leaders to read this chapter and engage in a dialogue with senior leaders about the topic of loyalty.
4. Review the three implications of the relational paradigm of loyalty. Which of these issues creates the biggest problem for your organization? What steps can you take to address this problem?

This content was originally posted as a Learning @ the Speed of Life vlog in June 2009.
To watch this vlog go to *www.TheMissionExchange.org/vlogArchives.php*

CHAPTER TEN
THE UN-PROVIDER: WHAT GOD MIGHT BE SAYING BY NOT PROVIDING

One of the most commonly referenced names for God in the Old Testament is Jehovah-jireh, The Lord will Provide. I'm sure you're familiar with the passage from Genesis 22, where Abraham is tested, facing a very difficult situation and at the last possible moment God intervened: God provided. Abraham was so moved by this experience he gave this place a new name, Jehovah-jireh. The scripture tells us a saying was birthed from Abraham's experience, "On the mountain of the LORD it will be provided." (Genesis 22:14)

As I interact with church and mission leaders during this difficult economic season, one of the most pertinent topics is the need for a fresh revelation of Jehovah-jireh. There is a lot about Abraham's story in Genesis 22 that we don't relate with but all of us can resonate with the fact that God provided at the last possible moment. I understand that sometimes God has to push my faith to the very edge, to stretch me to the breaking point in order to strip away my tendency toward human effort and to refine my character. But I wish every once in a while he would spare me the pressure and release provision some-time before the midnight hour.

It was obvious in the fall of 2008 that the economy was headed down and we were moving in to a challenging season for many churches and mission organizations. That's why we asked leaders in our sphere of influence to set aside the third Wednesday of each month during 2009 to pray and fast, asking God to give an abundant harvest in a season of famine.

In my days of prayer and fasting I sensed God is up to something in the midst of this difficult season. I've been intentional about asking God what He wants us to learn, recognizing wisdom is ultimately more valuable than money for effective leadership. While I was pondering this important question (God, what are You trying to teach us?) I came across a powerful idea in Craig Groeschel's book, *IT, How Churches and Leaders Can Get IT and Keep IT.* Here's what he said: "Maybe you've heard the old adage, 'Where God guides, he always provides.' We made up a new saying: 'God often guides by what he doesn't provide.'"[1]

That statement captured my imagination. I found myself ruminating about it for weeks. I modified it a little to say, sometimes God provides by not providing. It is not only counter-intuitive, it seems unbiblical. But listen to how Craig Groeschel unpacks his idea:

"Are you up against a wall with no good plan to get past it? Have you hit an obstacle that appears impenetrable? Maybe God will guide you to see something that you couldn't have seen if he'd just removed the wall."[2]

He goes on to illustrate this principle from the story of Peter and John at the temple in Acts 3. They encountered a crippled beggar who asked them for money, something Peter and John didn't have. Peter emphasized this in his response, saying, "Silver or gold I do not have, but"…and you know the significance of the rest of that verse. (Acts 3:6) So here's the question, what if Peter had a bag full of silver and gold? Can you see it? God provided for this crippled beggar by not providing.

In the midst of this season of financial pressure I've been asking God a simple question, "How might You be providing by not providing?" Or to use Craig Groeshel's phrase, how might God be guiding by not providing? I don't presume to speak for the North American mission community, but I do feel a responsibility as the leader of a mission association to think at a 50K foot level. So here are four big picture answers to these questions. I'm not offering these ideas as a word from God but rather as talking points for consideration. I'm not trying to convince you as much as I am to stimulate you to think along these lines for yourself.

1. *I believe God is pushing us into a new season of creativity and innovation.* Is it possible God might withhold financial resources to prod us toward new ways of thinking and doing that we would never even consider if our coffers were full? Maybe He wants to provide, well in to the future, by giving us new models, new structures, new paradigms for church and mission. All of our instincts when we are under-resourced are to hunker down, to circle the wagons. It will take courageous leadership to press forward and accept the risks associated with innovation in this challenging environment. How hard is God going to have to squeeze us before we get this?

---

[1] Craig Groeschel, *IT, How Churches and Leaders Can Get IT and Keep IT* (Grand Rapids, MI: Zondervan, 2008) location 1547 Kindle edition
[2] Ibid., location 1549 Kindle edition

2. *I believe God is calling us to much more partnership and collaboration.* We have heard people talking about partnership for years and there are exciting examples of this around the world. But I don't think we have come anywhere near the need or potential. For too many leaders partnership is a strategy, not a value, an expression of pragmatism but not principle. (More on this in Chapter 13.) Perhaps God is providing partnership opportunities for your organization you would not have entertained a few years ago. Maybe He is providing by not providing.

3. *I wonder if God is pressing us to explore what the business world describes as mergers and acquisitions.* Almost all mission leaders are convinced their organization is unique, doing something no one else is doing or in a way no one else is doing it or with a very important theological distinctive. But I wonder if God is trying to tell us there is too much redundancy and inefficiency, too many "me too" copycat initiatives. Maybe He is saying if some of us actually combined together we could do more than if we keep plodding along in the same direction separately. I believe one of the most important gifts to the ministry and mission world in the next few years will be godly consultants who can help churches and mission organizations merge. There are already some positive signs in this direction but I believe the real action is yet to come.

4. *Maybe God is nudging us to figure out how to gracefully walk through the closure and liquidation of some mission and ministry structures.* I know this will be difficult for some leaders to accept, but maybe some organizations have run their course. We often quote the phrase from the story of Esther, "for such a time as this." Is it possible "this time" has come and gone for some organizations? Is there really any disgrace in having the organizational self-awareness needed to close down with dignity?

Most board members succumb to subliminal group think within their first few meetings, believing their highest responsibility as a board is insuring the perpetuity of the organization. No wonder we become so risk averse and committed to our own distinctive identity. Maybe God is pressing us to figure out how to apply Acts 13:36 to mission structures, "For when David had served God's purpose in his own generation, he fell asleep."

It would be tragic to spend all of our energy during a season of financial duress trying to survive and not take the time or initiative needed to really explore how God might be guiding by not providing.

Something to think about, maybe even talk over with your team:

1. Almost every organization has historical markers that revolve around God's miraculous provision. What is your favorite story of this nature for the ministry in which you serve?
2. When we are facing a financial need our reflex response, understandably, is to ask God to provide. How might you seek to include a few moments (at least) of reflection in these circumstances to ask if God is trying to guide you by not providing for you?
3. What are some of the assumptions Christian leaders make (especially founders) about their ministry that could make it difficult to entertain a merger with another organization? If you were counseling a leader who was struggling to consider merging, what advice would you give?
4. Is it wise to assume that it is God's purpose for every Christian organization to continue to exist until Jesus returns? If no, how can we tell which ones should gracefully cease to exist? If you were a board member for a struggling church or mission what signs would you look for to suggest the possibility of closing the doors?

 This content was originally posted as a Learning @ the Speed of Life vlog in July 2009.
To watch this vlog go to *www.TheMissionExchange.org/vlogArchives.php*

 For more information on this topic, consider the following downloadable webinar in our online store at www.TheMissionExchange.org: *Mergers, Acquisitions and Alliances: An Introduction to the Possibilities and Processes*, by Scott Rodin, Managing Principal of OneAccord..

CHAPTER ELEVEN
MOVEMENT 2.0: THE NEW LEVERS OF SOCIAL CHANGE AND WHY YOU CAN'T IGNORE THEM

If you have been around leaders for very long you've probably heard someone describing an initiative he or she's involved in with a qualifying statement like this: "We are much more like a movement than an organization." This type of disclaimer is meant to suggest the leader is a structural minimalist, resisting the development of systems and policies in an attempt to empower grassroots activity, leverage influence and accelerate positive change.

There are usually two reasons for giving an initiative this kind of movement makeover. First, there are negative stigmas and stereotypes attached to institutions and organizations that some leaders want to avoid. Second, there is a recognition that decentralized, unstructured entities are more flexible and can leverage influence to produce positive change more quickly.

A lot of thinking and reflection has been done on movements over the years. One common explanation suggests creating a movement requires a man, a message or mission, materials, members and a meeting. (Sorry ladies, but you know how important alliteration is for this type of outline.) I believe that is a pretty accurate description of what used to be.

But the anatomy of a movement, what I'm calling movement 2.0 is changing. The primary influencers of social change in our flat and digital world will not be movements, at least not as we have understood them. But before I explain what is changing and why it's important, I want to give you a little more context for this discussion.

In general, throughout history there have been three basic levers of social change - institutions, organizations and movements. It is helpful to interact with these as not merely physical, structural or legal entities but also as paradigms or ways of thinking about how to influence others and initiate change.

Point leaders, the "man" of a movement, are still important, but in a flat and digital world the profile of a social maverick is changing. Being media and tech savvy can be just as important as old fashioned charisma and stage presence. Meetings and materials still have a role. But they are often even more effective as virtual instead of physical products. That's why I suggest it is now more accurate to think about levers of social change in the following categories: institutional, organizational, tribal and viral.

In other words, our digital and globalized world has created movement 2.0 in the form of tribal and viral initiatives. This is not just semantics and if you want to leverage your influence for positive change you have to understand these new realities as well as how to work with them. It will make you uncomfortable. It will challenge some of your deeply held assumptions about brand identity and quality control. The way forward is murky but I believe the leaders who figure this out will be the real influencers in the future.

I realize these labels, especially tribal and viral, will be new to some and ambiguous to others. So I want to take a moment to put all this in context. I want to do that by focusing on big picture generalities in three categories, looking at the structure, culture and posture of each of the four levers of social change, institutional, organizational, tribal and viral.

First, think with me about *the institutional lever*. The structure of institutions could be described as hierarchical. They are usually top down and protocol driven where people are rewarded for survival instead of performance, so working the system is a core competency in an institution.

When it comes to culture, institutions are bureaucratic. There are lots of committees, lots of red tape, plenty of emphasis on tradition. I describe the posture, how it presents itself, of the institutional lever as that of a defender. There is usually a hunker down mentality where value is placed on protecting something as opposed to inventing something. You might be thinking, "That sounds like our organization?" Then you are operating with an institutional paradigm. Remember, this is not only about physical or legal entities as much as a way of thinking that frames how you operate.

Second, in the *organizational lever*, the structure could be described as flexible. Organizations have an infrastructure but they are far more likely to add new departments or reshuffle teams than an institution.

When it comes to culture, while institutions are bureaucratic, organizations are systemic. Their policies and procedures are oriented more toward system-atizing activity in order to produce greater results than to preserve the past. So when it comes to the posture of the organizational lever, it is a producer rather than a defender. John Carver, in his seminal writing on board governance said, "The only justifiable reason for organizational existence is the production of worthwhile results."[1]

Third, the *tribal lever* for social change has a structure that is relational. It flows along natural lines of connection. Probably no one has championed the idea of tribes more than Seth Godin. He affirms "what people really want is the ability to connect to each other, not to companies. So the permission is used to build a tribe, to build people who want to hear from the organization because it helps them connect, it helps them find each other, it gives them a story to tell and something to talk about."[2]

The tribal lever of social change has a culture that is dynamic. It feeds off the energy and passion from other members of the tribe. It is a continuous cross pollination of ideas and opportunities within the boundaries of shared vision. I describe the posture of tribes with the word connector. And it is not primarily connecting them with an organization but with each other in the context of a shared passion. But if the passion of the tribe overlaps with the purpose of the organization there are powerful opportunities for collaboration.

Finally, there is what I refer to as the *viral lever* for social change. While the structure of institutions is hierarchical, organizations are flexible, tribes are re-lational, viruses are unmanageable. It is nearly impossible to predict who they will infect and how they will mutate. As a result, the culture of the viral lever is chaotic. It is difficult to control. I describe the posture of the viral lever with the word activator. If no one responds to viral initiatives, by default they don't become viral.

I realize I'm painting with broad brush strokes here and it's not really very important if you agree with the words I'm using to describe these four levers of social change. What is critical is that you understand the new movement, what I'm calling movement 2.0, will involve new realities of our global and digital world, specifically tribal and viral activities. It is not enough to understand they exist. We have to figure out how to collaborate with them and harness their power.

I believe the leaders who figure out how to engage movement 2.0 will be the pace setters and change drivers of the future. So let me give you some ideas to consider:

[1] John Carver, *Boards That Make a Difference* (San Francisco, CA: Jossey-Bass, 1997), 50
[2] blog post from January 30, 2008 - http://sethgodin.typepad.com/seths_blog/2008/01/tribal-manageme.html

1. *Figure out what it looks like to be viral friendly.* More specifically, learn how to give away your cause, to let others become advocates and activators. (See Chapter 7, The Power of Viral Ministry.) The pressing question will be, "How can we do this without compromising on quality or diluting our brand?" I'm not completely sure. This is where the water is still murky. Seth Godin would tell you the goal is not only to build a brand but to build a tribe and the two are not mutually exclusive, which brings me to my second idea to consider.

2. *Become tribal friendly.* Develop platforms that make it easy for people whose shared passion overlaps with your purpose to find and collaborate with each other. Don't try to control them; do try to influence them. How? By empowering them, serving them and by resourcing them. (This is a very different approach than simply asking them to resource you.)

3. *Become movement 2.0 savvy.* Understand that a powerful new lever for social change begins with viral activity; it grows thru tribal connectivity and is sustained by hybrid partnerships with organizations or even institutions to generate lasting productivity. Weaving together viral/tribal activity with organizational/institutional structures is messy and right now there are few if any widely accepted rules or models.

Going forward, a critical factor in leveraging social change (creating movements) will be understanding and refining principles and models for how to make these hybrid partnerships work, how to sustain them and how to multiply them. We need thought leaders who are willing to take the risk and accept the failures that will become the foundation for effectiveness in the future.

4 Levers of Social Change			
	Structure	**Culture**	**Posture**
Institutional	hierarchical	bureaucratic	defender
Organizational	flexible	systemic	producer
Tribal	relational	dynamic	connector
Viral	unmanageable	chaotic	activator

Something to think about, maybe even talk over with your team:

1. In order to embrace the viral and tribal aspects of movement 2.0 you will need to empower your constituents and "give your cause away." What are the primary limiting factors you will have to overcome in order to take this important step?
2. Review the paragraphs describing the tribal and viral levers. Which of the characteristics listed will conflict the most with your organizational culture? What ideas do you have about how to resolve these conflicts?
3. Make a list of movements you have encountered that have emerged since the turn of the century. Analyze them against the characteristics of movements "as we have known them" and the principles of movement 2.0. What do you learn from this exercise?
4. What are the most important steps you could take to form a tribe? What pockets of your constituency would be most responsive to this kind of initiative?is to ask God to provide. How might you seek to include a few moments

This content was originally posted as a Learning @ the Speed of Life vlog in August 2009.
To watch this vlog go to ***www.TheMissionExchange.org/vlogArchives.php***

If you want to explore this idea further I recommend Seth Godin's book, *Tribes, We Need You to Lead Us*.

CHAPTER TWELVE
SWARMING: WHAT IT IS AND WHY IT MATTERS

Recognizing we live in an upload world we put out a call in midsummer 2009 for guest video bloggers to submit articles for consideration to become the September 2009 vlog thought. Justin Long provided this thought provoking content that resonates with and reinforces the themes we have been developing and was gracious enough to allow the transcript for his vlog to be included in this book.

I watched the March 2009 video blog on the punkification of missions and realized my story is a bit like that. It starts in 2006, with my kids, while we were living in Southeast Asia. One day they came running, excitedly calling me to the front porch--where a dead lizard could be found. The ants were already beginning to nibble at the corpse. We had to run an errand so we just left it there. By the time we got back, the ants were swarming it in earnest. Fascinated, we decided to leave it overnight. By the next morning, the bones had been stripped clean.

I was reminded of Proverbs 6. I began studying ants in my spare time, reading everything I could about them. In the process I discovered there were many kinds of swarms in nature--and there were many people who were learning from swarms, and making their businesses swarmish. But it wasn't just a business case either.

In his great book, *Here Comes Everybody*, Clay Shirky explains the Birthday Paradox. If you have a group of twenty-five people or more, there is a better than fifty percent chance two of them will share a birthday. By the time you get fifty people together, the odds rise to about ninety percent. The paradox, however, explains why groups are difficult to manage. People don't just share birthdays. They share opinions--but not always the same opinions. And the more people you get together, the more relationships there are, opinions to be heard, ideas to be considered--it gets very time consuming and costly.

In the past often only organizations and governments could do things because it cost too much to get people organized. Companies excelled at organizing people in the same way that they used to organize trains--which is in fact where the first organization charts came from. People in turn were paid money to allow themselves to be managed. This was one of the primary costs of doing business. Organizations had to be careful not to be "in the red"--where the expense exceeded income. Ideally, they would not do something unless they believed a profit could be made. Cars were manufactured, television programs were produced, computers were created--but if something didn't generate money, it was less likely to get done.

People, however, are social creations. We don't want to just be managed consumers. We want to consume things together, share them, talk about them, laugh, cry, and enjoy life. For all of human history we've been connecting with each other--finding a way to pay the cost. Whether it be armies, or political campaigns against slavery, or religious orders, or youth movements, or social protests, or elite groups, or not-so-elite book clubs, or just raising a barn--we like to do things together.

When some bright souls connected computers together, and the Internet was born, we social creatures took to it like kids to cotton candy. And the tools it gave us were not just one-to-one or consumption tools: we soon discovered we could share with many people, talk with many people, create funny pictures and videos to email to people, and eventually this whole social ecosystem exploded into hundreds of millions of websites, over a billion users, and an immeasurable number of emails, groups, and the like. This was so important to us that we kept improving the tools: kept putting more power into ever smaller packages we could carry with us everywhere, until we ended up with enormous amounts of communication power in the palm of our hands.

And when all the sharing and talking threatened to overload us with information, we began building Internet-based tools to help us gather the conversations and organize them into easily browsed lists. We labeled these tools social media--tools that let us share. It was so useful that tools like Facebook grew explosively to over 250 million members. And a funny thing happened. Along the way we began organizing ourselves less and less in hierarchical charts and more and more according to relationships.

Now we are discovering that "zero" is different from "less." As our technology and our computing power increased, we began seeing certain costs--to organizing people, managing people--decline. When costs decline, two things happen for businesses. First, the biggest businesses, which are most efficient, get bigger (perhaps by gobbling up some less efficient businesses). Second, lots of little, nimble businesses move in to take advantage of the new more open space. But what happens when costs are shattered? when they drop from "less" to virtually "none"? Then something different happens. Now we have two lines. One is a green line: above it are the things people will pay for, and below it are the things people will not pay for. And we have the red line, far below, for the cost factor. There is a space of things that are so cheap that anyone can do them: if you care more about value than income.

Businesses and governments will not typically play in this space, because there is no income to be had, and for all their efficiency businesses still have administrative costs: legal registration, taxes to be filed, buildings to be paid for, and so on. But individuals and small groups of individuals don't have these costs. And thanks to new technologies--which have given us new ways of thinking--individuals can organize groups very cheaply, and can begin to do things on their own.

In 1999, Northwest Airlines had some flights snowed in. Passengers sat in the planes, just a few yards from their gate, for over eight hours, getting angrier minute by minute. One enterprising passenger got hold of the phone number for the president of Northwest Airlines, and called to complain. When they finally got to a gate, lawsuits were of course filed. But they were all settled out of court, and it all went away after a while. Epic waits were not unusual. Jetblue, too, once left a flight sitting on the tarmac for eleven hours on Valentine's Day. But in December 2006, American Airlines had a flight that sat for six hours, and this time it was different. Kate Hanni was on board, and when she got off she was mad as a hornet. But it wasn't Kate or her anger that made a difference. It was this: she wrote a lengthy comment about her experience on a news website, and invited people to contact her. When they did, they began organizing online. They gathered over 10,000 signatures to a petition and began lobbying Congress to enact a passenger's bill of rights. What made the difference between 1999 and 2006 was the ability to organize online, to connect, to share, to call attention, to plan action.

These kinds of quick, self-organized, self-led groups are what I call swarms. After studying example after example after example over the past four years, I've come up with seven key descriptions for them.

1. *Every swarm is focused on a specific goal which is often not market-related, and ruthlessly measures itself by that goal.*

2. *Every swarm organizes relationally and operates collaboratively.*

3. *Swarms tend to be low cost and sustainable because they are usually autonomous, unregistered, all-volunteer with few funds involved, and highly localized.*

4. *Through their activities swarms often completely transform the environment and culture that they live in.* Everyone is affected by what they do.

5. *Swarms are always experimenting, always trying new things out, always quick to adapt.* Since they don't have much in the way of resources they have to be very nimble around threats and opportunities.

6. *Swarms are often open and free--almost painfully so.* They use free resources and give stuff away for free, and we wonder how they "make ends meet." But swarms don't usually exist to make a profit. They want to achieve something of importance.

7. *Swarms multiply themselves.* They are usually attracted to a vision bigger than them, and while a swarm takes one tiny part of the vision, they encourage other swarms to form to take on other parts.

What does swarming have to do with missions? We already have a number of "mission swarms" in existence. YWAM is one huge swarm. Less known are how swarmish WEC and Wycliffe are. And there are thousands of little church-based ministries which have gotten an enormous boost from these tools.

Can swarming help your ministry? Yes. And the key is that you don't have to change overnight. You can start in little ways to be a little more swarmish and reap the benefits.

You can be more swarmish by clearly defining your goal and documenting the many ways you can reach it.

You can be more swarmish by developing ways to teach these goal-achieving actions to others.

You can be more swarmish by giving people some way to meet online, and talk about the goal, and how they are achieving it. Give them a platform to share what works and doesn't, successes and failures, encouragement and critique. Don't try to censor them--instead, be a servant.

You can be more swarmish by helping people form small local groups to teach others what they have learned.

You can be more swarmish by giving away resources to these groups for free--resources that will help them get better.

You can be more swarmish by listening to people whom you've taught, learning from their experiences, and sharing what you learn with others.

When you define a goal, gather people around it, organize them relation-ally, and help them work together to achieve the goal--a swarm is born. And it could just explode into something huge.

Something to think about, maybe even talk over with your team:

1. Where are you already engaged with a swarm personally but didn't even know it? How did you get involved?
2. What is the single biggest obstacle your organization faces to become more swarmish? How might you overcome it?
3. What program or initiative in your organization is most likely to attract a swarm? What is the most important next step?
4. Review the list of "little ways to be more...swarmish" on page 56. Which of these would be the most strategic step for your church or mission?

This content was originally posted as a Learning @ the Speed of Life vlog in September 2009.
To watch this vlog go to **www.TheMissionExchange.org/vlogArchives.php**

DEEPER

If you'd like to learn more about swarming and related ideas, Justin Long offer Swarming Seminars online (email justinlong@gmail.com) and more writings about swarming at www.strategicnetwork.org.

CHAPTER THIRTEEN
THE HOURGLASS EFFECT: WHY PARTNERSHIP MOMENTUM STALLS IN MIDDLE MANAGEMENT AND WHAT TO DO ABOUT IT

One of the most widely held core values for evangelical ministries in general and mission organizations in particular is partnership. Almost everyone acknowledges in one way or another that the Great Commission is too big for any one organization to do alone and too important for us not to try to do it together.

Our primary focus at The Mission Exchange, how we go about accomplishing our mission to increase the effectiveness of the Great Commission community, is by adding value to leaders and stimulating partnerships. These are the two filters we use to evaluate all the new ideas we process. In the few years I've been in this role, I've discovered that it is a lot easier to add value to leaders than it is to stimulate partnerships.

I realize partnership is hard work but there is a part of me that struggles to understand how so many organizations can say partnership is a core value and yet find the process of stimulating or initiating real collaboration is such an uphill climb. It makes me wonder if just maybe, for many organizations, partnership is more of a strategy we employ when we think it's appropriate than a core value by which we seek to consistently operate.

Let me try to illustrate what I mean with a computer metaphor. I suggest that core values are to an organization what an operating system is to a computer. It is the platform that is always running in the background. Strategies, and the methodologies that flow out of them, are to an organization what programs are to a computer. The program runs on top of and must be compatible with the operating system in order to function properly.

I'm suggesting one of the reasons partnership is such an uphill climb is because while we might describe it as a core value - part of our operating system, in reality it is more like a program we open when we think it can be useful.

One of the other observations I've made about the limiting factors that can slow down the momentum of a partnership is what I describe as the hourglass effect. You've seen an hourglass, it is wide at the top and the bottom but the shape of the glass narrows in the middle so only a small amount of sand can pass through.

I think that's a picture of what often happens with partnership. There is a general openness to partnership at the top of an organization with the CEO and senior leaders. You put some C-level leaders in a room together and the ideas start flowing, there is a sense of relationship, trust and camaraderie among them and at this big picture level there is often a very high receptivity for partnership.

A similar picture could be painted on the other end of the hourglass, at the grass roots level. This is especially true for mission organizations, where grass roots workers on the field engage in what I describe as micro-partnerships all the time as a normal course of their operations. In many cases these mirco-partnerships involve people from other mission organizations that would not normally be viewed as compatible by people in the home office or the support network.

The first time I encountered this dynamic at the micro-partnership level I was leading a team of young adults on a short-term mission trip in a country in South America. The missionary we were working with told me he would like to do an open air outreach that included showing a film but he did not have a projector or a generator at that location. He suggested we borrow what we needed from other missionaries and invited me to come along.

We went to one place and picked up the projector and a second place to get a generator. In each location he took the time to introduce me to the other workers and we talked briefly about their mission and the work they were doing. As we drove back to our home base I had this really awkward feeling rise up inside me because I knew the churches some of the students on our team were from would never do anything in their home towns in partnership with the denominations from which we had just borrowed the equipment. I rather awkwardly asked the missionary if he would be OK with not telling the team members where we got this equipment for fear they would tell people back home and I'd have to deal with the negative feedback. The missionary was very gracious, affirming he knew full well what I was feeling; we didn't tell the team where we got the equipment.

Let's come back to this visual I call the hourglass effect; it is wide at the top and the bottom but narrow in the middle. I believe one of the challenges of implementing partnership is middle management, not because the people who serve there are any less open to working with others than their senior leaders or grass roots colleagues, but because they are responsible for hashing out the details, and we all know who is in the details.

It is at this middle management level, in the center of the hourglass that we have to figure out how to collate all of our policies and procedures with the practical realities of doing something together that we would have otherwise done ourselves. And that's a real challenge. I believe it is the responsibility of senior leaders to help unclog, to open up the middle of the hourglass, by clearly articulating answers to the following six questions. If you are in the middle management of an organization and you don't know how your C-level leaders would respond to these questions (as it relates to specific partnerships) you have every right to press them for a clear response.

1. *Theology: How much of your theology do others need to agree with before you can partner with them?* I realize orthodoxy is important and as evangelical leaders we have to take this seriously. But remember, as you answer this question, unless you are prepared to say the people who don't agree with your doctrine will not make it to heaven, when you walk away from a partnership over doctrinal reasons, you are in effect saying, "I'm willing to worship with you in heaven for eternity but I'm not willing to work with you on earth now." I'm not saying you should never put yourself in that position. I am saying you should consider it carefully.

2. *Philosophy: How much of your philosophy of ministry do others need to agree with before you can partner with them?* I believe your philosophy of ministry is comprised of the principles and values that determine how you gain and use power, how you make decisions and how you evaluate success. You have to have an explicit understanding of your own philosophy of ministry and leadership, especially as it relates to how you evaluate success, before you can even begin to answer this question.

3. *Authority: How much authority, or we could say control, do others need to relinquish (in terms of decision making or finances) before you can partner with them?*

4. *Strategy: How much of your strategy— in terms of goals (what) and methods (how)— do others need to agree with before you can partner with them?*

5. *Publicity: How much of the publicity (in terms of promotional materials or progress reports) needs to have your corporate identity in order for you to partner with them?*

6. *Chemistry: How much of the other leader's (or team's or organization's) personality do you have to be compatible with in order for you to partner with them?*

Something to think about, maybe even talk over with your team:

1. Is partnership listed on your web site and promotional material as a core value for your organization? If yes, what evidence would you provide to show partnership is part of your operating system and not merely a program?
2. Think of a partnership opportunity that was derailed at the outset or grossly underachieved. Debrief the partnership using the six questions listed in this chapter. What did you learn from this exercise?
3. Identify a specific and significant partnership venture your organization is engaged with currently (or in the last year). How confident are you of the answers to the six questions that help "unclog the hourglass?"
4. Schedule a meeting with your senior leader(s) (or if you are a senior leader with your key middle managers) to discuss these six questions in relation to specific partnership opportunities ranging from evangelistic outreaches, to church planting, to mobilization initiatives, et cetera.

This content was originally posted as a Learning @ the Speed of Life vlog in October 2009.
To watch this vlog go to *www.TheMissionExchange.org/vlogArchives.php*

DEEPER

For more information on this topic, consider the downloadable webinars in our online store at www.TheMissionExchange.org: *Three Rails of Partnership* by Ellen Livingood, *Authentic Inter-Cultural Partnerships* by Daniel Rickett, *Partner Friendly Organizations* and *Results Focused Partnerships* by Brian O'Connell.

There is a practical and informative article by David Hacket, of visionSynergy, in the 2009-2010 edition of *eXcelerate* magazine, which is available in PDF format at www.TheMissionExchange.org. (Note in September 2010, this edition of *eXcelerate* will be moved to an archive page under the Get Connected, Award Nomination tab.)

CHAPTER FOURTEEN
RE-THINKING THE ISSUES OF FAITHFULNESS AND FRUITFULNESS

If you are a leader you are by default a philosopher and here's why. Your first order of priority is to define reality and a close second is to define success. So in spite of your bent toward action, before you can get practical you must first get existential by defining reality and philosophical by defining success.

This is a challenge for all leaders but I believe Christian leaders are faced with a unique set of limiting factors and are particularly vulnerable. First, when it comes to defining reality, Christian leaders are often tempted to "paint the sky blue" with optimistic projections of how God is going to "bless our ministry," ignoring or glossing over challenges that stand in the way. Please don't misunderstand me; faith in an omnipotent God is critical and leaders are called upon to model positivity. But emphasizing God is bigger than our challenges is not the same as pretending we don't have any challenges at all or that they are too small to justify a closer look.

Recently I had the privilege of interviewing Harvard Business Professor, John Kotter, about his book, *A Sense of Urgency*. Kotter shared about the amazing capacity of leaders to ignore trends and data that others outside the organization would view as powerful indicators of a crisis that demands a sense of urgency. His observations were not singling out Christian leaders but I believe Christ-following leaders are especially vulnerable to denying, or at least downsizing reality and we do so to our own peril.

Second, when it comes to defining success, Christian leaders often bristle with discomfort, believing it is difficult, perhaps impossible, to reduce kingdom activity down to data points that can fit on a spread sheet or monthly report. Skeptics make comments like, "Sure, we can count heads, including the people who 'respond' to our invitations. But how many of these people are nowhere to be found a month later? Does our counting tell us what really happened to them or more importantly "in them?"

One of my first and most formative experiences with defining success came about twenty years ago in a rural village of South India. I was leading a group of students serving alongside an indigenous Indian mission called India Gospel League. Our primary ministry focus was showing the Jesus film. It was an amazing experience. Lots of people, in some cases entire villages, came to watch the movie, which is based on the gospel of Luke. The message is powerful.

I'll never forget one of those first evenings after the movie was over and people were given the chance to come forward to receive prayer or ask questions. Many of them did. The ministry time was powerful. As the evening was wrapping up I asked one of the key Indian leaders how many people became Christ-followers that evening. I knew this mission was diligent about gathering statistical information about their ministry so I assumed he would be prepared to answer my question.

But instead of answering my question he graciously put me off. I thought perhaps he was too busy getting packed up and waited a few minutes before asking again. This process repeated itself several more times before finally my Indian brother pulled me aside and said, "Steve, whatever you know about evangelism and discipleship, forget it while you are here in India. It has nothing to do with our context." I'll have to admit that isn't what I was expecting to hear. And he could tell by the look on my face he had my attention.

He went on to explain to me that so far as they knew the village we visited that evening had been steeped in Hinduism for generations. Most likely everyone there was hearing the message of the gospel for the very first time. It simply wasn't possible to wipe away the deeply held worldview of these people in a few hours. He went on to explain that he could say with great confidence a church would be born in that village, building on our ministry that evening. I wanted him to tell me who would be in this gathered community but he simply couldn't.

He explained that over the next few weeks and months they would have a bare-foot pastor (that's their term not mine) return to the village to gather people who were interested to answer questions and continue studying the Bible. The result of that process would be a new church. I had about two hours of riding to get back to where we were staying and I mulled his words around in my mind the entire time.

That powerful experience taught me when it comes to metrics, context is critical as well as knowing what and when to measure and the importance of communicating accurately. I have developed a simple but powerful question that I believe zeros in on the leadership priority of defining reality and success:

If a primary stakeholder in your church or mission asked if you are making progress toward your vision and mission, assuming your answer is yes, what specific evidence would you reference to validate your answer?

That's a very important question and the only way I'm going to convince you to read it again is to print it again, so here goes:

If a primary stakeholder in your church or mission asked if you are making progress toward your vision and mission, assuming your answer is yes, what specific evidence would you reference to validate your answer?

Unless you are prepared to look your stakeholders in the eye and say, "It is not possible for us to know if we are moving in the direction of our vision and mission," you have to identify some metrics because if you say yes (or no for that matter) you have to have, either implicitly or explicitly, some point of reference that serves as the basis for your answer. Unless you are prepared to tell your stakeholders, "Stop asking this question because we can't and don't know..." deferring any answer until Jesus comes, you have to identify some metrics, some indicators of the outcomes connected with the bottom line of your vision and mission. And wrestling with the performance, or we could say success of your organization, will bring you face to face with reality.

There are some who would say, "Steve, wait just a minute." You are confusing two important but distinctly different ideas. You are confusing faithfulness with fruitfulness. Yes, we are called to be faithful, but only God can produce fruit. You can't hold me accountable for something that is out of my control."

This is a very important issue that deserves more than sound bite treatment in this short chapter. (I encourage you to take advantage of the resources in the Want to go deeper? section at the close of this chapter.) Too often faithfulness and fruitfulness are viewed as two ends of a continuum held in creative tension. A more helpful model is to view faithfulness and fruitfulness as part of one contiguous feedback loop.

You can't say you are truly faithful if you are not diligently seeking to grow your capacity, develop your giftedness and refine your strategy. Faithfulness goes so much deeper than just showing up. So at the heart of faithfulness we are constantly asking, "What could we be doing differently? Is there a better way?" These questions are only meaningful if linked to the other part of the feedback loop, fruitfulness, which asks the questions, "Are we bearing fruit? Much fruit? Lasting fruit?"

We fully understand the answers to these questions (Are we bearing fruit?) will always be incomplete on this side of eternity. God is at work in ways that go beyond our observation. But the fact the answers to these questions are incomplete does not render them unimportant. And no matter how much or how little the harvest, we ask ourselves, "What could we be doing differently to bear even more fruit?" Is there a better way?"

So let me go back to my reality-success question: If a primary stakeholder in your church or mission asked if you are making progress toward your vision and mission, assuming your answer is yes, what specific evidence would you reference to validate your answer? Whatever you reference, those are your metrics. Do they help you confront reality and define success? That's what good leaders do.

Something to think about, maybe even talk over with your team:

1. Where do you struggle most, defining reality or success? How has this affected your leadership effectiveness?
2. Reflect on a formative experience in your journey that shaped your beliefs about defining success. What lessons did you learn?
3. What biblical passages would you cite as having the greatest impact on your understanding of the relationship between faithfulness and fruitfulness? Why?
4. If a primary stakeholder in your church or mission asked if you are making progress toward your vision and mission, assuming your answer is yes, what specific evidence would you reference to validate your answer?

This content was originally posted as a Learning @ the Speed of Life vlog in November 2009.
To watch this vlog go to **www.TheMissionExchange.org/vlogArchives.php**

For more information on this topic, consider the following downloadable webinars in our online store at www.TheMissionExchange.org: *Metrics for Missions Conference Package*. This downloadable resource bundle includes a webinar entitled *ReThinking the Issues of Faithfulness and Fruitfulness* by Steve Moore, along with six additional webinars on *Results-Based Management* by Claudia Horn.

AFTERWORD

There has been a remnant of Christ-followers in every generation who believed they were running the anchor leg of human history and Jesus would return in their lifetime. Regardless of how long God will wait patiently, not wanting anyone to perish, I believe it is honoring to Him for us to live with a sense of passion and urgency about accelerating the fulfillment of the Great Commission among the only generation for which we will give account: this one.

When I first began to seriously study the Scriptures I was enthralled with the Gospels and Acts imagining (even wishing) what it would be like to have lived during that era of history. I would have conversations in my mind with the apostle Paul about how wonderful it must have been to witness the birthing of the church across cultural boundaries.

More recently I have come to believe the conversation with Paul might be quite different than I first imagined. I can hear him sharing how much he would have loved to live and serve at time when travel was so efficient, communication so instant and resources so plentiful. I can imagine his core leaders saying how much they longed for the "latter days" when God promised to pour out His Spirit in such unusual ways and how amazing it would have been to live among those to whom the baton of responsibility for the Great Commission was passed one last time.

Amidst all the urgency, uncertainty and vulnerability that comes with leading in this moment in history we are faced with unprecedented, perhaps never to be repeated opportunities. *God, please help us not to miss them.* Difficulties, complexity, even tragedy, are some of the most potent fertilizers for the soil of leadership. *God, please take our roots deeper and our branches higher.*

Jesus said:

"And this gospel of the kingdom will be preached in the whole world as a testimony to all nations, and then the end will come." (Matthew 24:14)

The writer of Hebrews said:

"For in just a very little while, 'He who is coming will come and not delay. But my righteous one will live by faith. And if he shrinks back, I will not be pleased with him.' But we are not of those who shrink back and are destroyed, but of those who believe and are saved." (Hebrews 10:38-39)

Some generation of Christ-followers will not merely read these words, they will live them out. If not us, then our children or children after them will know these words experientially. If our role is, like those before us, not to run the anchor leg but to pass the baton to a remnant that comes behind us, may we model for them a level of passion and commitment that fuels their resolve to "run in such a way as to get the prize." (1 Corinthians 9:24)

Let's continue this conversation…

If a few of these chapters have sparked fresh thoughts in your mind and you would like to continue the conversation I invite you to engage with me by way of the Learning @ the Speed of Life vlog posted on the fifth of every month at www.TheMissionExchange.org. If you want to be notified by email when a new vlog is posted all you have to do is create a profile on our web site. Click on the Log In tab on the top right hand side of the page, follow the link to the New Visitor Registration and complete the profile.

If you prefer you can simply utilize the RSS feed. But by creating a profile you will also be entered in our monthly drawing to give away a free book, free webinars and other resources we hope will help you keep Learning @ the Speed of Life!

HELPING MISSION ORGANIZATIONS **improve**

The brand promise of The Mission Exchange is increased effectiveness. We are committed to harnessing the collective wisdom and experience of the Great Commission community to help your organization do what God raised it up to do even better than it is now.

For the past few years we have worked diligently to deliver on our brand promise by adding value to individuals serving in mission organizations, both members and beyond. In addition to three live conferences, every year individuals serving with a member organization of The Mission Exchange have FREE access to 36 book summaries, 24 live webinars, 12 author interviews, and 6 Global Issues Updates. That includes every home office staff member and missionary anywhere in the world.

While we are excited about the progress we are making in adding value to individual mission leaders, we recognize to accomplish our vision and mission, to deliver on our brand promise, we need to provide a service that could help an entire organization become more effective.

improve: Feedback Driven Continuous Improvement

Over the past eighteen months we have been designing and testing a new service of The Mission Exchange called **improve**. It represents our commitment to deliver on our brand promise at the organizational level.

We built **improve** on the following five assumptions:

1. Leaders are stewards of a vision from God and will be held accountable
2. Every organization has room for improvement that would increase its effectiveness
3. Every leader has blind spots that limit and filter his/her perspective of what or how to improve
4. Some areas of improvement are more strategic than others, providing a greater return on investment
5. A proven approach to exposing blind spots and prioritizing action steps is objective feedback

improve is a flexible but systematic process that enables mission organizations to work with an organizational development consultant to process feedback from stakeholders, mission peers and an Executive Coach to develop a list of priority action steps to begin a journey of continuous improvement.

Your biggest problem as an organization may not be the one you can't solve but the one you can't see. That's why feedback is at the center of **improve**. The process is designed to expose organizational blind spots and shed light on new possibilities. It harnesses the collective wisdom and experience of trusted mission peers with outside objectivity who are empowered to ask probing questions as well as offer strategic counsel.

The Three Phases of improve

Phase 1 of **improve** provides feedback from stakeholders, both internally (your key leaders and management team) and externally (your donors, prayer partners, church partners and volunteer constituency). The internal stakeholder feedback comes in the form of an organizational self-assessment completed online in eight modules: 1) organizational & legal, 2) organizational identity, planning & governance, 3) human resources & team development, 4) finances, 5) marketing & communication, 6) technology, 7) innovation & change management, 8) partnership.

The external stakeholder feedback in Phase 1 is provided through a Constituent Engagement Survey that measures the four pillars of engagement: integrity, confidence, pride and passion. If your constituents trust you (integrity), and believe you are positioned well to accomplish your mission (confidence), they will have a sense of pride about associating with you and become passionate about your mission.

Data from Phase 1 is analyzed with input from an **improve** consultant to develop an initial list of Priority Action Steps. All the phase one information is communicated to a carefully selected group of mission peers for Phase 2. **Phase 2** of **improve** engages the input of three to five Christian leaders from the church, business and mission world, who have agreed to review Phase 1 data and participate in two virtual peer consultations. The first peer consultation asks, "What's happening now?" with a focus on strengths to build on and challenges to work on. The second peer consultation asks, "What's happening next?" with a focus on innovation and recalibration. After the second peer consultation the list of Priority Action Steps is updated, with the help of the **improve** consultant, in preparation for Phase 3 feedback.

Phase 3 of **improve** provides feedback from an Executive Coach directed to a point leader in the organization who will oversee the implementation of the Priority Action Steps. This three to six month coaching relationship is designed to shine the spotlight on the next steps that need to be taken in order to get out of the block with a healthy start, identifying key questions of application: what, who, how and when?

All three phases of **improve** are undergirded by prayer, asking: What is God saying? (Phase 1) What is God doing? (Phase 2) Where is God leading? (Phase 3).

The entire **improve** process is focused on four intended outcomes:
1. increased organizational self-awareness that produces
2. high ROI priority action steps that yield
3. increased organizational effectiveness, which contributes to
4. a culture of continuous improvement.

"Your biggest problem may not be the one you can't solve but the one you can't see."

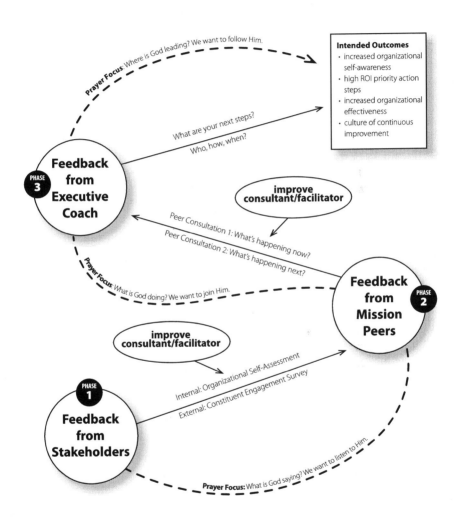

If you would like to explore how **improve** could help your organization become more effective, please contact us at improve@TheMissionExchange.org or 770-457-6677.

For an expanded list of frequently asked questions, visit our website at www.TheMissionExchange.org/improveproject.

A Word about Snowfall Press

Printing at the Speed of Life.

Life is changing at a relentlessly fast pace. And while many pundits rue the day when everyone read more and watched television less, they fail to understand that through email blasts and other social media sites luminaries such as Guy Kawasaki and Seth Godin are streaming nearly non-stop content focused, in large part, on keeping their RSS feed audiences up-to-date with the nuances of the changing face of technology and the world in general.

Between hundreds of emails each day and the constant stream, and mosquito-like annoyance, of instant messages demanding their attention, people are actually reading more now than ever. But rather than reading for pleasure, reading has become a manic attempt to stay current with changing elements of their profession and the world in general. Reading is work.

Steve Moore deftly shows us this rapid, constant change is ubiquitous and crosses into all professions and personal lives. You keep up or you face becoming irrelevant. That is certainly true in the book printing, publishing and distribution industry.

As Steve indicates in Chapter 1 much of what we knew about getting a book published has changed already. A new model has been needed for some time which would present content in a more user oriented fashion, and get the content to people where they are and when they need it. As you will recount, Steve called it Gutenberg on steroids – and he is right. And that solution exists right now.

Snowfall Press has developed an innovative printing process that allows content of all kinds, from publishers, mission organizations, or even individual authors to be developed into a book, even for small groups of readers and make it available worldwide…at very low cost per book. In fact, Snowfall is so economical, anyone can print just one book if they want – it is that cost-effective.

And just like Gutenberg, Snowfall had its start in printing Bibles in low quantities - on demand. Founder Todd Tillinghast noted several years ago that there was a lot of Bible translation activity worldwide, translating the Bible into local languages of many obscure tribes all over the world. And after so much work was put into years of translation, it would be hard to get funding for the print run. Economics dictated that several thousand of those Bibles would be printed. The reality was sometimes only hundreds were needed. The results were either boxes of Bibles languishing in someone's closet or the translation did not happen at all. Tillinghast did not think this was right and set about to fix this dilemma. People were skeptical about the probability of Tillinghast (and Snowfall's) success, but not only has Snowfall been successful at printing Bibles, particularly Bibles on thin paper, but they created the first fully-integrated and automatic book printing solution and have gone on to enable Christian authors and publishers to more economically bring all kinds of books to market.

For instance, as Snowfall grows, publishers and authors will be able to utilize the growing network of print nodes around the world to print books only where they are needed and when they are needed, keeping distribution and storage costs to a minimum. Imagine needing 100 books printed but knowing when they were completed 25 would need to go to the UK, 25 would be heading to Colombia, and the rest would be shipped in the United States. With Snowfall's distributive print solution, the books going to the UK and Colombia would be automatically printed simultaneously in those countries – saving shipping, importation taxes and the capriciousness of customs officials in some countries.

But even today, using the Snowfall Solution, which includes no set-up charges or minimum run commitments, publishers can bring new authors on-board with confidence - knowing they can be profitable even when running small initial book runs to test market the author's viability. Authors too can take full advantage of Snowfall's technology. Whether an aspiring author or one who has been publishing for years, there are no set up fees and no minimum book runs –saving lots of upfront fees.

Plus, as Steve noted, those books would not even be printed until paid for and then shipped directly to the end-user reader - ensuring the publisher or author does not have to warehouse books. In fact, because the books are not even printed until they are sold, the classic print burdens of unsold books or returns are done away with as well.

A good example of using this solution is from Brent Lindquist, president of

Link Care Center in Fresno, California. Because it is so economical to print books in small print runs, Brent wrote a book in under two weeks and incorporated his handouts along with a full color laminated cover, and used that for a small conference where he was speaker for less than the cost to go to a commercial photocopy service.

And that has been the experience of many people in ministry – compare the costs of printing a workbook at your local copy/air delivery service company to Snowfall's prices and you see how a quality book printed by Snowfall is cheaper than a copied and corner-stapled version.

Christians should be at the forefront of these changes

Snowfall Press enables individual authors or mission organizations to easily utilize this technology.

One organization plumbing the depths of this new book printing technology is Initialmedia. Run by Anton Smeele, Managing Director, Initialmedia has a vast network of mission and church organizations around the world (US, Europe and Asia), that want to have all their printed material managed through one source – including the design, marketing, production and distribution of these materials. "When I first met Brent Lindquist over a year ago at a conference in Thailand," recounts Smeele, "I knew the book printing solution he was describing was a perfect fit for servicing many mission and church organizations (captive markets) around the globe. Snowfall Press and Initialmedia began a long-term relationship to facilitate the various needs within the networks. (Anton Smeele can be contacted at anton.smeele@initialmedia.com.)